THE ROMANTIC IDEAL

The Highest Standard of Romance for a Man

Also by Gregory V. Diehl

Brand Identity Breakthrough

Travel as Transformation

The Influential Author

The Heroic and Exceptional Minority

Everyone Is an Entrepreneur

Our Global Lingua Franca

Courage to Live

THE ROMANTIC IDEAL

The Highest Standard of Romance for a Man

A Hopeless Romantic's Exploration of Masculine Intimacy, Sex, and Love

By Gregory V. Diehl
With a Feminine Foreword by Svetlana Sevak, MA, RP

IDENTITY PUBLICATIONS

For permission requests, write to the publisher at contact@identitypublications. com.

Library of Congress Control Number: 2024921900

Orders by U.S. trade bookstores and wholesalers. Please contact Identity Publications: Tel: (805) 259-3724 or visit www.IdentityPublications.com.

ISBN-13: 978-1-945884-93-1 (ebook)
ISBN-13: 978-1-945884-94-8 (paperback)
ISBN-13: 978-1-945884-95-5 (hardcover)

First Edition, published in Buffalo, Wyoming, by Identity Publications (www.IdentityPublications.com).

Cover by Safa Azar (www.SafaAzar.com).

DEDICATION

When a man reaches the edges of where his perspective will take him on its own, the smartest thing he can do is hand his thoughts over to the right woman to pick apart and play with in her complementary fashion.

Important parts of this book are the direct result of long conversations I had with Svetlana Sevak—a beautiful and self-expressed woman who, due to our uncanny psychological chemistry, forced or allowed me to go deeper into what I was trying to explain about things nearly unexplainable. Her incessant questioning and uncommon ability to articulate her feminine perspective on things I thought I understood forced me to improve the scope and depth of what I had to say about being a man and loving a woman or being a woman and loving a man.

She was the only person appropriate to write the foreword you're about to read. In a way, she co-created this book with me, acting in part as a mother to the ideological offspring I was father to in what eventually grew up to be this book.

TABLE OF CONTENTS

FOREWORD

In my practice as a trauma therapist, I have noticed an interesting trend with every patient I've worked with. There have always been prominent relationship issues present in their personal lives. No one has ever come into my office to address other issues who didn't also have serious relationship issues. People who came to me with self-esteem and body image issues turned out to have communication problems with their partners, for instance. Some people came to me suffering from anxiety after traumatic accidents, only to eventually reveal that the hardest thing they were dealing with was that their partner was not caring enough during their rehabilitation, which was more hurtful to them than the actual injuries they dealt with.

It is very unfortunate that knowledge about gender differences and relationship dynamics between men and women is not widespread because it results in a range of personal problems and disorders (or exacerbates unrelated ones). It seems to me that the majority of people nowadays are so concerned with seeing equality in everything that they have forgotten about seeing equity, which is where we all meet each other's needs and feel valued, respected, and accepted for who we are as individuals in the highest possible way.

Compared to men, who are more single-tasked, women have a stronger ability to quickly switch between their right and left lobes in the brain or even have them activated simultaneously. Consequently, they are better able to perceive and process emotion and logic, coming to conclusions quickly and calling it a

gut feeling (a.k.a. "women's intuition"), which can feel alien to men, who feel that women can be poor at rationally assessing how they decided something so quickly or explaining their conclusions in explicit terms men will understand. I consider myself hypersensitive to this facet of feminine nature. My professional training in classical singing, particularly in the art of opera, has polished my mastery of simultaneously activating logic and emotion and elevated it into a complex system of self-awareness. My unique engagement in operatic art and psychotherapy has resulted in a highly personal journey of observing, analyzing, and understanding myself as a woman, and I have placed a high priority on assessing my feminine experience of life rationally and coherently for men and women alike.

The author of this book is a highly intellectual man who, for as long as I have known him, has been in a state of constant self-development. I can say with a high degree of confidence that his number one goal in life is to help people understand important things, in his signature style, that they cannot easily learn about from any other source. It requires a huge amount of self-awareness and self-study to notice every mistake, every imperfect facet of the past, as the author has attempted to do for himself, and make a public statement and choice about how he wants to grow from it and the man he aspires to be.

Though this book is written from a very personalized masculine perspective, bravely provided by Gregory V. Diehl, I believe it is a huge step forward for people to learn healthy relationship dynamics, understand fundamental differences between men and women, and accept that gender dynamics are a vitally important and inseparable part of our lives that cannot be avoided. In that regard, it is similar to learning about health, finances, or the environment. We can sit in ignorance and pretend it does not personally affect us or matter much in the grand scheme, but we will pay the price for our ignorance of the principles at play in our lives. The author has undertaken a monumental task by self-analyzing and reflecting on his own experiences and comparing them with permanent fixtures in global human mythology. He has a preternatural talent for educating and expressing the complex and incomprehensible as comprehensibly as possible to the public.

This book shows that there are certain qualities that highly masculine men desperately need from highly feminine women (and vice versa). These qualities and the need for them reveal the essence of true masculinity and femininity. In the 21st century, virtually everything is available to everyone. Anyone can do almost anything on their own. A single man can have his single life happily with access to basically everything they could ever want. Likewise, a single woman can live a fully functional life without a man. Each can even conceive and raise children without the support of the other. So why do we still crave each other?

Men have always sought (and, I believe, always will seek) certain feminine characteristics that exist most prominently in women, and women seek certain masculine characteristics that exist most prominently in men. And it's okay to need each other. Eventually, we *should* need each other. If we want to reach a divine level of human connection, if we want to reach something very sacred, we have to like and love needing each other. Celebrating the differences between them is the best way that men and women can achieve harmony together. As such, this book will make women feel good about being needed by men, and the same with men being needed by women for the respective duties and responsibilities they seek to offer in a romantic partnership.

Nowadays, it's often misinterpreted as a bad thing, as a great insult, when you tell a woman she needs a man (or even that a man needs her). It's a very damaged mentality to be offended at the idea of needing your complementary influence or being needed to provide complementary influence to someone else. I can understand the author's lamentation that people have misinterpreted and been offended by some of the ideas contained in this book, even ones that were clearly meant as empowering and complimentary. Our respective roles go much deeper than how most people interpret them in the most superficial sense.

From this book, men will learn that women are not just beautiful objects (as the author calls them) or innocent creatures that exist to entertain, serve, and arouse them without volition of their own. Women will learn that men can be irresponsible and disregard vital things in relationships in a way that is alien to them. They will also learn that, despite how it might seem, there are good, highly masculine men oriented toward romance who are ready to commit and sacrifice everything for the right feminine influence from a good woman. Masculine dedication and love should not be underestimated or taken for granted by women. Indeed, wise and smart women will never be indifferent to that magical masculine magnetic force that attracts and is attracted to its much-needed femininity.

As women, we need to understand that men are very easy to deal with once we can look at them from a detached and realistic angle and try to understand who they truly are and what they truly need from us. Typical masculine men have certain systems and identifiable logic behind every single action, thought, and behavior. These stay quite stable throughout their lives and will not be changed unless something malfunctions. Men like to speak to already tested scientific methods, things they know work. In contrast, typical feminine women make ongoing changes and decisions, derived from their highly intuitive nature to better things and fully experience every emotion possible. To men, this often looks like unpredictable chaos.

The burden faced by feminine women is our way of constant questioning and self-criticism, which contributes to our more erratic nature. A woman faces a lifelong social burden of constantly being at the center of attention as an attractive human being. With that comes expectations for who she is supposed to be, how she is supposed to look, and how she is supposed to act. We always feel like we are under surveillance. Everybody's looking at us under the world's largest magnifying glass. We also have a more fearful nature than men. It comes from insecurity and the constant need for protection, which are qualities that are also socially reinforced in most societies. We attempt to fix this by surrounding ourselves with supportive people who give us a sense of security and protection from outside ourselves. If we cannot build that sense of security internally, we start overdeveloping our masculine side instead of feeling free to express our femininity.

When a woman brings chaos into a romantic relationship, a state of being the author refers to as "the feminine minefield," it's because of how insecure she feels in her relationship or life. She does not know who she is for her partner. A woman needs to feel comfortable and know who she is in this man's life with high security. Otherwise, she can become chaotic. She's looking for her protector. When she doesn't have someone who can protect her emotionally, give direction, or just confirm what's happening, she becomes like a tornado.

Women thrive in rest and beauty compared to men, who thrive in action and achievement. Men work to become someone attractive to women because they are not born the type of gentleman every

feminine woman dreams about at least once in her life. Men learn to be gentlemen either from observing male mentors or by being motivated by feminine women holding them to such a standard. There should be some type of grand motivation for a man to act and grow into the man he should be. A man being a gentleman means choosing to become full of thoughtfulness, desire, and consideration toward the woman he is most attracted to, in a way he never cared to pay attention to before, by channeling such core masculine qualities as ambition, protection, and leadership. I believe this is what the author refers to as the type of feminine qualities masculine men allow themselves to develop that are attractive to women.

In our very complex and chaotic world, being gentlemanly is often mistaken for spending an unreasonable amount of materialistic fortune in a performative way, which you will see the author criticize several times as an indicator of a performative relationship or pseudo-romance. However, I see it as a man being confident enough to showcase this very sexy and subtle masculine behavior, which can be materialistic but is not necessarily so. It demonstrates his creativity, intelligence, commitment, and bravery. This is undeniably attractive and heroic to feminine and self-satisfied women. Two people become more emotionally sensitive and attentive as a result of gentlemanly behavior and, consequently, connected. Since women observe, notice, and feel everything at a more sensitive level, these thoughtful moments initiated by a man cannot go unnoticed. Consistency of gentlemanly behavior will make a woman become more trustful toward a particular man and react favorably to his behavior.

Men are very lazy beings in general, which makes them oriented toward efficiency of action. They need justification for putting effort into things. "Why should I do that? Why?

What's the purpose?" The women they desire set the standard for coming out of that comfort zone, for setting higher standards and maturing. The author expresses this principle under the heading *Men Can't Live Up to Their Masculine Potential Without Women* in chapter two as part of what he considers to be a woman's signature influence on a man. The way I see it, every man is a Lego® set that needs to be assembled, rather than the already assembled model that most women expect to meet. A wise woman should learn how to identify the quality of the blocks and whether the set has all the parts needed. This is true feminine happiness. The author claims these women "want to skip ahead to the finish line" instead of playing their important feminine role in a man's masculine development. Indeed, the courtship process is the path to a strong relationship because it allows men and women to build a strong influence on each other and develop together into their potential, meaning men and women need to know how to provide positive emotions outside of the sexual context before feeling comfortable with the physical act of sex.

Men seldom realize that sex for a woman happens in the brain before the body. It's a moment of rapid dopamine and oxytocin release, which women can get even without physical stimulation. Events such as shopping, having a "beauty day," taking care of a child, enjoying a dinner or dessert, or simply being complimented by strangers can initiate this dopamine stimulation. Talking with someone they feel they can trust can be like sex to women because of the intimate connection they feel. They can talk, feel heard, and feel safe with a gentleman. Thus, they can share all their thoughts without being judged. As the author details in chapter four, *The Sexual Burden*, "Feminine comfort comes from knowing what to expect. Knowing what to expect makes her less hesitant to express herself in a sexually dynamic way." Women can start talking to a man and then become detached from this world because of how safe they feel. They don't have to edit their thoughts or words. This is the whole essence of masculine protection on a very profound but non-evident level.

Therefore, to get what she wants from a man, a woman needs to be very skilled at communicating her sexual and other needs. Sexual communication comes after being able to communicate all types of wants and wishes in life and after having established all ways of communicating with a man. Plenty of relationships collapse because there is no established method of sexual communication. There is no openness. There is no trust because people are afraid of each other's reactions. Women and men need to learn how to give and receive positive emotions to and from each other outside of the sexual context. A woman seeks someone who can listen and understand her, which she perceives as protecting her emotionally. She will do everything to find such a soul in a man. And if she cannot find that in her partner, she will replace him with a psychologist or by having an emotional affair with another man who is open to listening to her.

Very often, romantic love is mistaken for that heightened hormonal state of being physically attracted to someone from first sight, which usually sacrifices the opportunity to learn about the person the way they are. It happens in opposite sequences for men and women. Men get attracted by female looks, and they decide to approach her. Later, they realize that she is more than a beautiful object. She has a brain in her head, and maybe they have romantic chemistry beyond the physical. Meanwhile, a woman is initially attracted to the brain of a man, and later, she realizes that they also have a physical connection and lets herself feel sexual lust for him once she is comfortable.

Understanding a man is the main mission for a woman considering marrying and spending her life with him. Marriage is the highest emotional institution for highly feminine women, requiring absolute levels of commitment, responsibility, and attraction. If she feels that she understands this man and that this man matches her ideals, she can fall in love with him. In fact, it's a lot more work for a woman to find someone she can trust and express herself completely with than men can imagine. That's the goal for a woman: to find someone she can build trust with intellectually, physically, and emotionally in all possible ways. That's where security comes from.

I hope my contribution of a more feminine interpretation to the author's highly masculine one provides some balance and validation to the idea that there is a great deal for men to learn about women, women to learn about men, and everyone to learn more about themselves in the pages that follow. Gregory has taken great trouble to detail the masculine experience of intimacy, sex, and love in a way that will speak quite deeply to a certain type of reader, regardless of their gender. It is my ambition to undertake a similar feat in a forthcoming book of my own that explores the essential feminine side of these important topics and more, providing the complementary perspective that his idiosyncratic take is missing.

Written by Svetlana Sevak, MA, RP
Registered Psychotherapist
Toronto, Canada

INTRODUCTION

There has probably never been a major civilization in history that did not have a strong conception of the gendered differences between men and women and how they applied in a cosmic way. It goes much deeper than, for instance, the domestic rules imposed on women and career freedoms allotted to men in 1950s America. Cultural, philosophical, spiritual, and religious associations of men, women, masculinity, and femininity can be found at virtually any time and in any place that one is willing to look.

Archetypal contrasts demonstrate the universal human tendency to understand the world through the lens of complementary opposites such as up and down, light and dark, hot and cold, active and passive, and (drum roll please...) *masculine and feminine*. The obvious example is the ancient Chinese concept of yin and yang, represented by the iconic symbol of a circle divided into two swirling halves of black and white. In Hinduism, Shakti represents the feminine, dynamic, and ever-changing aspect of existence, and Shiva is the masculine, conscious, and unchanging one. Ideas about the "divine masculine" and "divine feminine" appear throughout various iterations of New Age spirituality. Psychologist Carl Jung developed the concepts of anima and animus to describe his ideas about the opposite-gendered influence subconsciously present in men and women, emphasizing that integration between the two was necessary for self-realization.

Of course, the fact that an idea has had a history of being popular does not constitute a logical argument or offer proof of its validity. It does, however, mean we cannot be quick to dismiss the differences between men and women as some recent, superficial blip on the radar of humanity's understanding of itself. If homo sapiens was not a sexually dimorphic species, we would not need complementary categories to understand and classify ourselves by gender besides the physical differences in our downstairs plumbing. Because males and females are different in many notable ways, our minds have come up with distinct methods of associating them. Beyond the sex organs, there are several important distinctions between males and females of most species on this planet. Naturally, our minds start categorizing those traits found more prominently in men as belonging to a "manly" category and those found more prominently in women as belonging to its complementary opposite.

Beyond the social reinforcement of gender roles and limitations, there exists a natural biological and psychological division of traits[1] between the sexes—and it's a good thing so long as we can arrange things so that our respective strengths work in each other's favor. Instead, the male/female dichotomy has often been embodied as a fight for control, each side employing strategies suited to their strengths. Problems arise when we stereotype and prescribe these traits, shaming men for not embodying the furthest possible extreme of masculinity and women the same for femininity. Because most men naturally

---

1   *Many will recognize "division of labor" as an economics term that refers to how any process is most efficient if you separate types of value according to who is best suited to provide each. Sexually dimorphic organisms, like people, have unevenly distributed traits between their sexes, from the functions their bodies perform to how they think and feel. Each approach provides some natural advantage the other lacks.*

grow more body and facial hair after puberty than women, we might too quickly conclude that women having any body hair makes them masculine or that men not growing enough body hair makes them feminine. The same applies to various personality differences that might be more likely to show up in men or women and that we, therefore, come to associate as masculine or feminine ways of thinking, feeling, and acting.

Though this book primarily addresses the masculine experience, it is intended for everyone. It's for men, of course, to understand themselves better—to find healthy ways to deal with what they are experiencing or likely to experience throughout life as a masculine entity. Many unhealthy habits we've stereotyped and socially accepted (and even disastrously encouraged) about men are things we can learn to deal with more responsibly. For women, this book aims to shed light on what the men in their lives endure so that they can better empathize with and support them. Feminine women frequently underestimate how the masculine experience of life can be so different than what they experience. It will also help them know what qualities to look for in good men and be confident about how men should treat them.

As I can't claim to know what it's like to be a woman directly, everything I write about women and femininity comes from informed guesses and an external masculine perspective, not personal experience. I can only infer certain principles about the feminine experience and compare them to my lived experience of the masculine one. When the woman who wrote the foreword to this book, Svetlana Sevak, finishes her similarly themed book from the feminine perspective, I'll be the first to read it. I suggest every man and woman reading this book does so, too.

The behaviors and experiences I describe in this book are, so far as I can discern, part of the quintessential masculine experience.

If you are actively embodying your masculinity (even if you are female), you should recognize the principle in yourself and see how it applies across your lifestyle, including how the failure to apply it leads to struggle and unfulfillment. Your life will be harder than it needs to be if you fail to embody who you are at your core, and you will not feel at home in yourself. Not every man is going to be horny all the time. Not every man is going to view sex and women the same way. Not every man is going to deal with his anger by punching holes in drywall, which would be a clear sign of immature masculinity and the inability to manage masculine frustration. It doesn't make me any less of a man if I don't watch sports, drink beer with the boys every weekend, get into bar fights, or go out hunting for pussy. I experience the same impulses that other men do. The difference is what I do with them. Being a man does not have to mean glorifying the worst things about men just because they set them apart from women. I hope to offer a superior, positive alternative to addressing the masculine burdens of existence.

For whatever reason, masculine traits are naturally overrepresented in men and feminine traits in women. If they are the product of our evolution, experts more qualified than me can only speculate about the advantages they've provided that have led to their proliferation in our species. Though the potential for endless diversity and individuation exists and should be respected, there are still broad categories of personality, values, and experience that most people will primarily identify with. Most masculine men are attracted primarily to feminine women, and most feminine women are attracted primarily to masculine men, for instance. Both natural genetic/hormonal expression and social conditioning likely play significant roles in this—though that's not a can of worms I'm ready to open here. Still, neither masculinity nor femininity is exclusive to men or women. If you don't feel like you belong squarely in the categories I describe, apply your own judgment and self-analysis to see how what I am talking about could still broadly apply outside of you.

Most people probably wouldn't think me to be particularly masculine from afar. I'm average height with a slim build (though I can put on muscle when I try to). I'm not excessively hairy, I don't have a square jawline, and I can't even grow a decent beard. But my personality, the mind that sees the world and makes sense of all its workings, my default emotional responses to sensory experience, my orientation to reality, and the types of goals that bring meaning to my life are almost entirely masculine. My weaknesses and failings are masculine, too. My experience of the world is alien to most women, especially those who are inversely skewed toward the feminine, just as their experience is alien to me. The further we stray in either direction from the neutral androgynous center, the more important it is that we understand and empathize with each other to reap the benefits of our respective strengths and specializations.

I've written this book at age 35—a nice, level station from which to assess my own experience of masculine development thus far. I've been an adult man long enough to have settled into it, past the chaotic sensitivity and hyperactivity of my teenage and early adulthood years. I've seen how my sexual interest and masculine demeanor have stabilized over time. I haven't yet experienced the decline I anticipate will come in my twilight years as I descend into being what I imagine as a helpless curmudgeon, when my hair goes gray, and I lose much of the virility that presently defines my experience as a man.

Throughout this book, I'll address pertinent examples from my own detailed romantic experience in cultures worldwide that primarily influenced how I formed my present worldview in this domain. All personal anecdotes included really happened. However, except for public figures who have freely disclosed their private details, names and details have been changed and mythologized to protect anonymity while getting the point of each story across. The lesson contained in each matters more than the specifics of what occurred. I will also draw on many examples from ancient and modern mythology and philosophy, usually in the form of parables, movies, books, and music, that illustrate timeless archetypes and truths about gendered romantic experience better than could ever be captured by something that just so happened to happen to me or someone I know. Though these examples do not offer scientific truth, they demonstrate that these ideas have been floating around in human culture and mythology throughout history. That's the point of mythology: to showcase a concentration of the most important aspects of the truth that are normally hidden from view.

APPEARANCES OF SEXISM

While writing this book, I'd occasionally come across someone who seemed offended by its very premise. Some people took issue with me not only *acknowledging* the differences between men and women but actually *promoting* them as qualities worth celebrating in pursuit of total self-expression and social harmony,[2] likely because they saw them only as sources of historical conflict and strife. Male readers would often praise me for the passages denouncing toxic feminine behavior but take offense at the

---

2 *"Social harmony," as I use the term, means individuals getting along with one another once they are self-expressed. We can ignore historical examples of totalitarians and social engineers using "social harmony" as justification for forcing people into roles to fit their particular vision for civilization.*

passages denouncing toxic masculine behavior. Female readers frequently did the opposite: They thanked me for shedding light on how men mistreat them and became volatile when reading about how their own sex is often responsible for mistreating men. It would be easy to take certain portions of this book out of context to make the person who wrote them look like a diehard misandrist or misogynist. This is a book that has to be interpreted holistically to receive it as intended. If you find yourself getting offended when I generalize and criticize aspects of your gender and not just as much when I do so with the opposite gender, ask yourself why.

Men and women alike have the capacity to be despicable creatures, though typically in different ways that are manifestations of their immature masculinity and femininity, respectively. Which gender we're allowed to criticize more harshly seems to change with the times. Personally, I am an equal-opportunity hater. I am quick to criticize all things worth criticizing and call all spades spades, disregarding momentary cultural narratives around these things. At my core, I'm a timeless humanist[3]—a universal champion for conscious self-expression in whatever form consciousness is to be found: male, female, big, small, round, square, and any color of the light spectrum. I know that everyone who does not radically assess their capacity for acting irresponsibly threatens everyone they interact with. And everyone who harms another when such harm was reasonably

---

3 *I would argue, though, that even the term "humanist" is an oversimplification of my position. I value humanity because it contains the highest concentration of certain virtues in the known universe, such as emotional depth, intelligence, morality, consciousness, and volition. My bias toward humans would naturally extend toward any other beings, now or in the future, who display such human-affiliated qualities, which we might broadly refer to as their capacity for humanity. Perhaps a more appropriate term for me than "humanist" would be "humanityist."*

preventable should be held accountable. If you feel called out by condemnations of certain negative gendered behaviors, ask why you identified yourself in them.

Any advice presented in this book is only valid if following it would be an authentic expression of the self in each reader's particular case. This is a disclaimer that, realistically, should be included in any book written in the genre of personal or sociological development. Any book that appears to tell you who you should be or how you should act only makes sense if those instructions are in line with who you really are. No one has the authority to try to change someone into something they are not.

The Semantics of Generalization

The English language is pretty bad at distinguishing generalizations and absolutisms.[4] It is the difference between when something happens *often* and when something happens *always* by definition. When Isaac Newton said that an object in motion remains in motion until an outside force acts on that object, he meant that it was true for *all* physical objects and *all* forces. It's part of what defines them. But if I say that men are physically stronger than women, I clearly don't intend to apply the claim on an absolute scale to *all* men and *all* women as a facet of their definition. I mean that it is generally true, even if I don't explicitly say so. We have enough data about men and women to broadly describe the scientifically informed sexually dimorphic differences between them. Beyond what we can directly confirm as laws and hard statistics with experimentation via the scientific method, we must venture into the weeds of philosophy, personal experience, and interpretation. That men and women

---

4   *In fact, as far as I am aware, no world languages contain a clear grammatical distinction between statements meant to be interpreted generally and absolutely. They all require additional semantic distinctions that can muddle meaning when such distinctions are left out.*

are demonstrably different in a variety of biological and psychological aspects is a scientifically informed conclusion— one that goes well beyond the scope of this book. However, what it *means* to be masculine or feminine and how men and women can best express themselves and get along together is a matter of personal values and interpretation.

Imagine the chore of reading a book semantically required to include the qualifier "generally speaking" in every sentence. My solution is to apply generalization as a disclaimer unless statements are clearly emphasized as absolutisms. Every claim I make about men and women in this book is intended as broad generalization, and most generalizations are descriptive, not prescriptive. I am not usually saying that things *should* be the way I portray them here. I am describing what I observe, the truth as I understand it. My wording should make it clear when I am projecting a preference or ideal instead of describing a fact. Perhaps your observations and understanding differ. Perhaps you can read mine and still gain something from them.

Generalizations are not stereotypes by necessity. A generalization is a pattern you identify that broadly categorizes your experiences. A stereotype is a generalization you apply *before* experience because someone passed it on to you. They, too, most likely had it passed to them via reports from others, biasing their interpretations of their experience. Sometimes, the patterns we identify from our experiences can align with existing stereotypes. Ironically, we might deny what we observe as true because we are extra cautious against being influenced by stereotypes. We stop trusting the evidence of our senses and our own ability to reason, which is the best we have in the absence of hard scientific data. Just because people think something is true doesn't mean it *is* true. It doesn't mean it *isn't* true, either.

CHAPTER 1

The Highest Standard of Romance

The subject of this book is idealism in a particular domain of life: romance and everything connected to it—namely, intimacy, sex, and love. Idealism consciously upholds a standard of the highest possible good. If you're a romantically oriented individual, you will, by default, be seeking out a certain type of influence in another person that you can't get anywhere else. It's a form of inherent passion. Romantic love is love defined by passion more than any other kind of love. Some people are born passionate about animals. Some people are born passionate about music. They naturally gravitate toward it or anything related. You can love your friends and family, but that's not a love typically defined by passion. Passion is something that burns inside. It has an intrinsic fuel supply that never runs out so long as you are alive because it is a consequence of your design. It would be very harmful to

tell someone to ignore any kind of authentic passion, to try to pretend it doesn't exist because it's risky or inconvenient or because it seems incompatible with their environment.

A romantic idealist (or, in my case, a romantic iDiehlist) faces a difficult time finding someone who lives up to their romantic ideals. And even if, by some miracle, you meet someone who has the potential to fit the bill, there's still a whole heroic journey you have to go on together to make that relationship work at a level beyond basic compatibility. It's not enough to win the lottery by finding the right person. You have to invest your winnings well and manage your wealth for life.

Romantics are brought into this world feeling a certain undeniable burden at their core. They carry it their whole lives and have likely always been aware of it. For many, society told them they would outgrow it and lower their idealistic standards to match the conditions of "the real world" everyone else lives in. I'm an idealist in many ways besides my orientation toward romance. I want world peace—a complete and permanent end to all war. Does that sound idealistic? Utterly impractical? Like something that would never ever happen, dooming me to disappointment? World peace is my ideal. If we can get even a little closer to that, I will be a little bit happier. But until we reach that ideal, I will still be disappointed with the state of the world. And such idealists are virtually guaranteed to see their ideals fail to actualize. "Disappointed idealist" is a cliché for a reason.

Every great artist who's ever lived and every person who's ever championed an important cause has known the pain of idealism. They were tortured by an idea, a standard that burned in their head. They had to paint some incredible vision or fight some great injustice in their time. They had to change the world because reality was inadequate for them. Even the ones who died before the work was done may still have made a meaningful impact across generations. They made progress easier for those who came after. We have all benefited from the suffering of idealists who did not sacrifice their principles. Their reward came from the work itself, knowing that there was a chance all their effort might make a difference one day. It could, eventually, change some lives. It could go on to create something that didn't exist before, something that once seemed impossible.

Love does not have to hurt, but for the romantic idealist, it is likely to. Unmet expectations hurt, and love in its ideal form requires the setting of extremely high expectations. The test of idealism is if enduring all the pain and disappointment is worth it in the end. If you're the kind of person who would willingly jump back into hell for a chance at making it work and finally getting what you know you want and need to be fulfilled, you're an idealist. I'm a romantic idealist who has repeatedly failed at enacting his romantic ideals—yet, against all odds, I have resisted the descent into romantic cynicism. I remain hopeful about and dedicated to the fulfillment of the standard I have set for myself about how romantic love will define my life.

"Scratch any cynic and you will find a disappointed idealist."

— George Carlin

People typically love the idea of love, the performance around love, more than the real thing. They cherish the gestures and symbols associated with it. If you really feel it, the symbols become superfluous. It's like a painting of a sunset compared to the real thing. It's just a visual reminder of something incredible. And there's no harm in having that unless you start to mistake it for the real thing. If you love someone, there's nothing wrong with buying them flowers. But the love and the feelings associated with those flowers are not dependent upon the act itself. And you don't have to default to flowers as the symbol of your love just because it's common. You should do it because you know your lover actually appreciates flowers. Does the emotion of romantic connection exist independently of the gestures? Would it persist without them as a product of two romantic individuals' unique chemistry?

Love songs, love stories, love letters, bouquets of flowers, and expensive diamond rings[5] are the sort of things non-romantics fill their conscious experience with to feel like they are participating in the illuminating dance of genuine intimacy. They need a constant resupply of these symbols for fear that the "magic" in their romantic relationships will run out. They feel only just enough of the hunger that they seek out a mere representation of what would actually satiate them. Such performative romantics will often be disappointed by real romance. It can never live up to all the pomp and hyperbole of the imagery derived from it, imagery that no longer accurately captures it. So, on they go, living in an invented world that has less and less to do with true romantic bonding. They are children playing dress-up compared to real adults who embrace the responsibilities of the real world.

---

5   *Actually, the wedding ring might be the only romantic symbol that makes any kind of non-arbitrary sense to me. It's a social signal to let potential suitors know not to get their hopes up about romancing someone already pair-bonded. However, the elaborate and expensive form they have come to take, such as the arbitrary insistence of spending three months' salary on one, is more about indulging in a status symbol established by a manipulative marketing campaign.*

They are geeks cosplaying as their favorite comic book characters. LARPers[6] who have lost sight of what they are supposed to be role-playing—illusion without any connection to the real.

All types of love are shared identification with another being. Parents love their children to the point that their survival instincts extend to them. Friends and comrades bond over shared support, pastimes, and values. But romantics seek to merge both body and identity with the one they love. It is like a natural chemical reaction that automatically occurs when they are near the person they are most romantically compatible with. The extreme end of natural romantic compatibility is the ever-elusive, much-fabled "soulmate," which does not have to mean the one-and-only great love that two people are predestined for from birth. A naturalistic explanation works fine, too. Soulmates are people who have the rarest and highest capacity for romantic bonding due to their complementary nature.[7] They fill each other's needs so strongly that it nullifies their tendency to seek out alternatives. However, it is not a foregone conclusion that they will find one another and put the work and growth into making their ideal relationship work. Both must embrace their nature as romantics and seek the highest form of their self-expression, which they know is found in one another.

---

6 *"LARPers" is short for "Live Action Role-Players," actors who participate in interactive storytelling by pretending to be characters in a fictional or historical scenario.*

7 *The concept of a soulmate, if interpreted liberally, can extend beyond the romantic and even human domain. My cat soulmate was a sweet, petite, blind, dilute calico named Matit. She became the standard through which I evaluated my relationship with all other felines because of how, by pure accident, our natures were so utterly, magically, miraculously complementary. She needed exactly me, and I needed exactly her for us to become the most expressed versions of ourselves.*

Romantics are more sensitive to the bonding mechanisms between compatible lovers. It becomes an overlay for their experience of the world, related to an intuitive sense that your life, your ability to live out your identity to the fullest, is incomplete so long as it is missing the influence of the feminine (if you are masculine) or the masculine (if you are feminine). While non-romantics can casually ignore the half they are missing, romantics cannot. Hungry creatures are impelled to find food. Those in the cold and dark await the coming sun or huddle around the fire for vital warmth. Romantic people recognize that there is a better, upgraded version of themselves, their fundamental potential, waiting for them when they bond with the right person—and that the same divine luxury awaits the person they bond with. A romantic man is chronically burdened, and he cannot remove the burden on his own, no matter how smart or capable he pushes himself to become. He needs *her*. He needs the influence he finds only in *her*.

Romanticism results from acknowledging the natural imbalance in one's soul and all the limitations that come with it. Two people imbalanced in complementary ways create romantic polarity—the eternal, exciting, sacred dance between a man embodying his masculinity and a woman embodying her femininity. If everyone were eternally balanced, androgynous, and neutral, there would be no drive to bond with one's reciprocal. People who fall under this description may have never really understood why romance is so important to some people. Regardless, they have much to gain from learning what the experience is like for diehard romantics.

The ideal outcome of romantic love is a specific, elaborate, sophisticated state of being that's incredibly rare in the universe. It only occurs under just the right conditions for it. And maybe you can sustain it if you're very smart, very determined, and very emotionally mature. Most people have to search their whole lives to figure out what is capable of making them truly happy. Romantics are lucky in that regard. They already know what they need. They just face the mountainous task of making it happen without falling into the trap of mistaking a false or unhealthy bond for the real thing.

The love story most associated with the NBC sitcom *Friends* is, undoubtedly, that of unconfident nerd Ross Geller and preppy "girl next door" Rachel Green. Their on-screen will-they-won't-they romance spanned from 1994 to 2004 and inspired many shallow romantic tropes that still show up across television genres. The show ends on what it frames as the climax and culmination of their chronically on-and-off relationship, with Rachel famously getting off the plane that would have taken her out of Ross' life to pursue her dream job in Paris. Instead, she decides that *this time*, things will finally work out for them, despite them having tried and failed so many times before, to the point of already having broken up and gotten back together several times, been married and divorced, had a baby they raise separately, and ruined each other's attempts at relationships with new people. Has there ever been a more toxic on-screen relationship that refused to end?

On the same show, the understated friendship-gradually-turned-romance of sarcastic Chandler Bing and high-strung Monica Geller stands in direct contrast as a heroic and healthy partnership. Each member of the partnership is deeply flawed but compensates for the other's weaknesses with their strengths. Because they have spent years developing affection for one another as close friends, once they allow themselves to recognize their great physical chemistry, their romantic feelings quickly propagate into love that results in enduring marriage. As

complementary opposites, could they *be* any more perfect for one another? If *Friends* had been a more mythological show, Chandler and Monica would have been its romantic focus. Ross and Rachel would have been framed as a failed, codependent[8] romance that nobody should aspire to, and their story would have ended with the two of them growing mature enough to wish each other well as they went their separate ways.

> *"If I'm the best, it's only because you've made me the best."*
>
> — Chandler Bing to Monica Geller, *Friends*

Someone unsatisfied with themselves does not have a whole and sustainable identity. They should not pair-bond[9] with anyone, or they will forever be trying to compensate for what they have not developed within themselves. People can spend their lives chasing after satisfaction in infinite, invalid ways if they don't take the time to critically assess what kind of person they would have to be to feel like they are embodying who they truly are. People have to work very hard to develop their character, to approve of, at the deepest level, the people they are. Even after all that important

---

8   *Codependence is a psychological and behavioral condition wherein one person enables another's dysfunctional behaviors to the detriment of both people, characterized by reliance on others for approval, validation, and a sense of identity.*

9   *"Pair-bonding" is a term from evolutionary and social biology that refers to a strong and sustained connection between two individuals of a species, instigated and maintained by recurring hormonal reactions in each other's presence. In the context of human romantic relationships, it usually means sexual monogamy and lifelong commitment to aid in our prolonged period of child-rearing, which is one of the bases for our traditional conception of marriage.*

work, they could remain far from *fulfilled* as romantically oriented individuals if they cannot yet partake in the actions, the external accomplishments that would give them the sense of meaning they require. There is no further work they can do on themselves to create fulfillment. They have to venture out into the universe and apply themselves out there.

Conscious unfulfillment drives people to do incredible things. A man who is happy alone has no reason to seek out his soulmate and build his relationship with her. But for the romantically oriented man, his relationship is his life's great work of art. His Sistine Chapel. His Statue of David. His Mona Lisa. Life-changing romance, the kind people write love songs about and recreate in cultural mythology, is vital to the pursuit of his conception of fulfillment. It would be paradoxical to insist such a man achieve this before entering into a romantic relationship because building that relationship *is* what brings him fulfillment. It would require him to consciously deny the truth of who he is.

However, even for the most romantic man in the world, his romantic life cannot be the *only* thing that brings him fulfillment. There has to be something else he considers all-important, something worth pursuing throughout his life. The right woman embodies his love and acts as a mechanism through which he pursues everything else important to him (and what she respects and loves him for). He does the best he can in those areas, even while single and alone, operating at a fraction of his potential before he finds the love of his life. A man whose whole life revolves around *only* his woman becomes a needy, codependent puppy in her eyes. No woman wants that in a man unless she's a narcissistic manipulator.

Why should it be so difficult for a compatible man and woman to come together and fulfill their mutual wants in the domain

of romance? Why is falling in love with and marrying the right person seen as one of modern life's most difficult (but most essential) tasks? Most people are not clear on who they are and what they want. Romance of the right caliber is one aspect of full self-expression, and most people fail at expressing who they really are. Various fears and insecurities keep them from ascending to everything they are capable of, especially when doing so would go against the social order they are part of. Romantic bonding requires the conquering of all fears and insecurities that would prevent it. It requires two independent people to become the masters of their own lives and willfully choose each other as the expansion of their self-expression.

Still, it often seems that a codependent relationship built on personal weakness and undeveloped identity has almost everything in common, on the surface, with a healthy, self-actualized one. Our timeless love songs frequently boast about needing someone, belonging to someone, feeling lost or helpless without someone, living for someone, and so on. Are these healthy or unhealthy sentiments to express about another person? These words could be seen as cries of desperation, obsession, and unhealthy connection. When Daniel Cleaver told Bridget Jones, "If I can't make it with you, then I can't make it with anyone,"[10] he could have meant, "I love you so much that I could never be with anyone after you. No one else would ever compare to you." But it could also be: "I'm so incapable of being in a healthy relationship that it's hopeless for me unless you continue giving me a chance."

The healthy version of romantic love, the one we celebrate the world over, is the consequence of a complementary man and woman's mutual self-actualization. It's what both truly want,

---

10 *From Sharon Maquire's movie adaptation of Bridget Jones's Diary by Helen Fielding (Penguin Books, 1999).*

and it's heroic to put forth the effort to make it happen in spite of everything working against it. The unhealthy codependent version is the consequence of failure to fully integrate oneself. You desperately seek something inauthentic to you because it distracts you from the awareness of your inadequacies. That's how love turns into manipulation for one or both parties. Ideally, our loving expressions would display our willing interdependence upon one another. I trust you, and you trust me like no other, even though we are each vulnerable enough to be destroyed by the other. We are one because we are both better that way—the best we could ever be in these bodies, with these identities, here in this time on this Earth.

To deny the natural drives, passions, and values within us would be to deny and defeat ourselves. To be true to ourselves is to acknowledge the principle of who we are, even (perhaps especially) when those fundamental truths about the self distress us because we cannot fully embody and express them. Bonding with the right woman is how the romantic man fully expresses himself because of the signature influence she has on him, that magical quality he can never find anywhere else in the universe, no matter the depth of his other accomplishments.

CHAPTER 2

Woman's Signature Influence on Man

"To a great extent, the level of any civilization is the level of its womanhood. When a man loves a woman, he has to become worthy of her. The higher her virtue, the more noble her character, the more devoted she is to truth, justice, goodness, the more a man has to aspire to be worthy of her."

— Fulton J. Sheen, *Life Is Worth Living*
(McGraw-Hill Book Company, 1953)

The gendered dichotomy gives women and men notably different orientations to reality, different ways of relating to it. Femininity is oriented around experience, and masculinity around conception. A woman is a noun, a man is a verb, and every coherent sentence requires both a subject and a predicate. A woman has to *exist* in a certain state, and a man has to *do* something he considers meaningful. A consequence of this is that a man is so far removed from experience, so lost in his head thinking, that the only things that bring him into his body, into experience, besides the deepest losses, are moments of the most profound joy and beauty. The beauty of the right woman is the highest concentration of these virtues the romantically oriented man can know. Masculinity optimizes itself for a *conceived* purpose. The *meaning* a man ascribes to his actions is more important than any momentary *experience* of comfort or discomfort. He cannot directly experience the world except through the filter of thought. A woman, meanwhile, being experience embodied, usually can't imagine how hard it can be for a man to just *be*... and be content with *being*. He needs to qualify his being somehow.

Still, even the most masculine of men will have certain experiences that activate their potential for joy and beauty in the moment of experience—the black seed of yin in an otherwise white yang personality. For me, it's teaching children and taking care of animals like stray cats that bring out that bit of soft femininity. Some basic part of me is nurturing and caretaking of a quality it sees in innocent, developing lifeforms. It's my strongest feminine virtue. For women, it's attractive when a man *can* be feminine like this, not when he *must* be feminine. Every woman I've been involved with has been attracted to how I am with cats and children. But these feminine features are only attractive because I'm *not* feminine at my core. They are complements to an otherwise masculine persona. If I were feminine at my core, women would see me as, essentially, another woman. There could be no polarity, no romantic dynamic between us. But if I have a foundation in masculinity and can still show these feminine qualities when it's appropriate, it's the most attractive I can be.

In the same way, if women have their foundation in femininity but are not totally helpless when it comes to certain masculine virtues, that's attractive to men. You show what you're capable of beyond just what you are obviously, naturally good at. Anyone who over-specializes in any domain is a liability. If you cannot do anything that falls outside of your narrow gendered purview, you have a crippling weakness. You need to be taken care of constantly because life is a multidisciplinary affair that requires both extremes (and everything in between). If, for instance, a woman can analyze her own feelings in a masculine, detached, objective, and conceptual way instead of *only* in the deeply invested subjective and experiential feminine one, she is less volatile to herself and the bond of their relationship. The ideal pairing for a feminine woman who is in touch with her masculine side is a masculine man who is in touch with his feminine side. She doesn't *need* him to be feminine because she already does that so much better herself. Still, she wants to see that he *can* be soft and nurturing, for instance, if the situation calls for it. And masculine men, more than anything else, need women who can confidently embody their femininity for the wholly unique influence it brings them.

WHY A FISH NEEDS WATER[11]

I once assigned an English class to watch *A Man Called Otto*, the Americanized English film adaptation of the book *A Man Called Ove* (Atria Books, 2012) by Swedish author Fredrick Backman. Otto Anderson is a smart, practical, successful, mature, and helpful old man. He has lived a good life by his own assessment. But due to the untimely death of his wife Sonya, he lacks the crucial component that made his life worth living: a place to belong in the world, his doorway to experiencing all its beauty. And so, all the goodness he is capable of distorts into malaise and

---

11 *"A woman needs a man like a fish needs a bicycle" is a feminist slogan popularized by Gloria Steinem in the 1960s that challenges traditional notions about the dependency of women on men, insisting that men would be as absurdly un-useful to them as bicycles to fish. In contrast, a romantic man needs his woman like a fish needs water—something essential to its survival, functioning, and comfort.*

alienation from the world. He becomes determined to end his own life rather than continue it alone.

My students understood why losing the love of his life had put Otto in such a precarious existential position. But one question I asked stumped them: "What if Otto were a woman who lost her husband? Can you imagine the movie happening the way it did if the genders were reversed? Can you picture the women you know losing all sense of meaning and beauty in life at the passing of their husbands?" None could. It did not fit their intuitive paradigm of prototypical masculine and feminine personalities. The women they knew would be more likely to still have a fulfilling experience of life just by living, even alone. But for the men they knew, that might not be enough on its own. Men, unlike women, have to qualify their existence.

Sometimes, a man has too much to offer and no connection to the world. Sometimes, he is only underutilized potential. It is through the context of people he cares about that his perspective and skills gain subjective value. Otto's was a life surrounded by color that he intellectually understood but that he could not see or directly experience without the right catalyst. Like every masculine man, he required a special witness to his virtue. It mattered to *him* only when it mattered to *her*. The only thing that solved his suicidal ideation in the end was not being useful to other people but being accepted and integrated as a member of a new family, providing the sense of belonging he lost at the passing of his wife.

"*My life was black and white before Sonya. She was the color... She was a force of nature.*"

— Otto Anderson, *A Man Called Otto*

The movie *Me Before You*, based on the novel by Jojo Moyes (Penguin Books, 2012), follows newly quadriplegic banker Will Traynor as he bargains with his parents for the medical right to end his now unhappy life. Their last-ditch effort to change his mind about euthanasia, to get him to see the beauty and joy in life again despite his limitations, is to hire bubbly and beautiful Louisa Clark as his caregiver. Their secret hope is that the feminine charms and virtues she exudes will be enough to emotionally engage him in the act of living again.

Will is a man who has become (almost literally) disembodied by whole-body paralysis. He has lost his connection to the physical world. He is detached masculinity in the cosmic void of his own mind and nowhere else. Louisa is his last hope of feeling like he belongs here in the physical world again. A purely masculine experience of reality like his is devoid of the majority of beauty in all things. Women embodying their femininity bring the experience of the beauty, comfort, and grace of the rest of the universe into men's lives. Without beauty, there is no emotional connection to the world or any actions within it. Therefore, there is no motivation to do anything, to continue living at all. When I was actively suicidal[12] and considering the merit of terminating my life on an almost daily basis, one of the only things that brought temporary relief was the presence of women who bathed my life in their light and glory. Most of them had no idea the power they held, the power to sustain life itself when it seemed hellbent on ending itself. Sometimes, it was through sex and other forms of physical intimacy... but more often it was just by these lovely feminine creatures complementing my experience of life with theirs.

---

12   *A subject explored in greater detail in my forthcoming book on suicidal ideation derived from ideological sources, working title: Courage to Live. Look it up.*

Imagine living in such a world without beauty—to live in the world and know that it is beautiful but not feel emotionally connected to its beauty. What might that do to someone? Picture a whole world of night, darkness, and cold. Out there, in the distance, you sense the coming warmth and light as the shine of an impossible sun rises to meet you for the first time in so long that you can barely remember it. In those moments, it becomes your conscious and exclusive goal to pursue that warmth and light, as the comfort it brings is incomparable to even the best that the darkness before could ever offer you. That's the experience of the romantically oriented man falling in love with the right woman after a prolonged period of disconnect: like the sun rising, at last, for the first time at the end of a long winter. Like there were birds all around but he never heard them at all. Woman is the window to all the beauty in the world for him. More than that, she *is* all the beauty in the world for him, granting fluidity to his experience, taking him out of his head just a bit and putting him at home in the rest of his body.

A man is at peace when he is in love and filled with the beauty his love brings him. At virtually all other times, he fights battles and seeks out problems to resolve. The first glimpses of this peace might come only in the moments following sex and orgasm, even with someone he is not in love with. For a short time, his body is concerned with only the buildup of pleasure and its dissipation. No action is needed, or scarcely even possible, in this state. When a man has someone he loves, the mere fact of her existence and his knowledge of her place in his life can be enough to instigate a similar but prolonged state of contentment. She rescues him from the torment of his lonely existence by complementing it with hers. Perhaps, if such a romantic man should find his woman and a place to exist in this world with her, he will settle into a comfortable role, a place to belong that secures him in it before he floats away into the cosmic void. But if he should find only alienation from and rejection by all the beauty in the world, he will relegate himself to a mystic, permanently disconnected from the world because it is the only peace he can find on his own.

I know beauty exists, but most of the time, I cannot see it. I cannot feel it inside me. There is a chemical reaction that ought to be taking place, and its yield would be the most wonderful feeling in the world, but it has no catalyst. There is a world of experience that I am prevented from living in by a barrier I cannot label. All that I know is that there are two worlds: the one I live in and the one that contains all else. Women are motivating factors for men to break through that barrier and cross the threshold between conception and experience. Every time I have started falling in love with a woman, I have found myself silently pleading, "Is this it? Is it finally over?" I don't think that's a state the feminine soul can fully envision. Existence as toil by default. Friction. Work to begrudgingly carry on with for as long as can be managed. And all this struggle without reward depletes a man eventually. What good is it defeating dragons without a princess to rescue in the end?

In the long-running BBC show *Doctor Who*, The Doctor, an alien thousands of years old, travels the universe in despondent solitude whenever he is not graced by the presence of a (usually young and female) human companion. His plucky Earth girl pal is there to remind him of the inherent beauty of life and the goodness the world is capable of. She brings the alien down to Earth, so to speak.

The Last Temptation of Christ, the polarizing Martin Scorsese film, is noteworthy for depicting a flawed, human, and, at times, broken version of a divine masculine figure normally portrayed as unwavering and perfect. This film's Jesus is a man overwhelmed by the burden of his role. He is caught between the "spirit" (the masculine) and the "flesh" (the feminine), which is represented literally by his attraction to Mary Magdalene and his desire to forsake his destiny on the cross as the savior of mankind for a life of earthly pleasures with her. Even she, however, is ultimately only a representation of the principle of woman and what it means for this tragic masculine figure: the continuation of life in all its glory compared to death and the loss of everything worth living for. Embracing crucifixion in the end (spoiler alert) is a sign of his ascension to the person he was born to be. But importantly, he could only do so after synthesizing his two sides by fully exploring both over the course of the story's departure from the gospel version of events.

> *"Only one woman exists in this world, one woman with countless faces."*
> — Christ's Guardian Angel, *The Last Temptation* by Nikos Kazantzakis (Simon & Shuster, 1960)

Woman is the romantic man's source of integration with the world, giving him the chance to become an embodied part of it. Without her, he is isolated and estranged. He has no inherent reason to care about what happens here. He is a minimalist at his core, naturally disconnected from most experience. She is the catalyst that activates his ambition, drawing out his full potential because she gives him a reason to endure the suffering that accompanies it. Otherwise, when he compares himself to the world at large, he feels that he will always be viewing it from afar, never fully a part of it. He does not have any reason to believe that any coming moment will be any different from what he has endured so far. But the force of the woman so beautiful to him that he cannot ignore her is strong enough to pull him out of this state. She is a representation of life itself and everything good the universe can offer—everything that makes the suffering of a disconnected spirit worthwhile. The right woman rescues a man from the burden of being himself by being a doorway to the universe all around him.

MEN CAN'T LIVE UP TO THEIR MASCULINE POTENTIAL WITHOUT WOMEN

Many women exclusively want to date the paragon man who is already at the end of his masculine developmental journey, when he is more wealthy, established, mature, and secure. Yet, the majority of these women are still in the developmental state of little girls. They want the work to already be done by the time they join up with a champion. They want to skip ahead to the finish line, never realizing they are supposed to play an integral part in the ascension. The fusion of man and woman, the masculine and its reciprocal feminine, creates supermen out of men and chosen ones out of ordinary people. *He* can't be who he is supposed to be without her also being who *she* is supposed to be. A man only embraces his potential when he seeks to become worthy of the version of himself he sees reflected in the eyes of the woman who loves him. To embody his values, requires the strongest conviction, which involves both experience and conception—a strong emotion tied to a strong idea. It's like sex in his brain, a holistic union between the feminine and masculine within him. Suddenly, all his parts are working together for a clear and shared goal.

Auteur filmmaker Zack Snyder showcased the masculine spiritual conflict his version of Superman would face in *Man of Steel*. This is a version of Superman struggling to bridge the gap between man and super, unready to embrace the weight of who he is until receiving support from the right woman. This depiction of Clark Kent is depressed, unsure of himself, and operating at a fraction of his heroic potential. It's not until he meets love interest Lois Lane that he starts to believe he can be more than what he has been. He is even willing to die to protect his once-estranged planet because she becomes, to him, a representative of it. She's the entire world anthropomorphized. She is everything worth saving. The right woman who believes in him gives man context for all his strength and superpowers. Imagine how much more ordinary, how much less *super* he would have been without that.

> *"Thank you... For believing in me."*
> *"Didn't make much difference in the end."*
> *"It did to me."*
>
> — Superman and Lois Lane, *Man of Steel*

There's a similar often overlooked plot point from the Wachowskis' *The Matrix*. For most of the movie, Neo is not actually The One, the all-powerful savior of humanity from the machines that enslave it. He's still just Thomas Anderson playing dress-up in a black leather trench coat. It's not simply a matter of believing in himself, as we might see in a less romantic story. He had to be killed and then reborn with Trinity as his romantic partner—his other half. He could not be whole (or "one") without her. Her realization of her love for him and overcoming her apprehension toward *her responsibility to him* gave him the strength to transcend his human boundaries.

"Neo, I'm not afraid anymore. The Oracle told me that I would fall in love and that that man, the man who I loved, would be The One."

— Trinity, *The Matrix*

The alternative, the consequence for repeatedly failing at intimacy, sex, and love, might be that a man becomes the opposite of what he could be: the absolute worst version of himself instead of the best. The incel (short for "involuntary celibate") social trope captures the disastrous condition of men frustrated by their inability to act on their driving romantic and sexual impulses. Their stunted personality development and social functioning are obvious. But despite the modern terminology, incels aren't a new phenomenon. There have always been men suffering at the bottom of society's sexual and relationship hierarchy. Men who never learn how to navigate the romantic expectations of women and attract compatible sexual partners are condemned to horrid, sexless lives lacking the majority of the beauty the world can offer. It doesn't have to be a man who has never been able to procure sex from women despite years of fruitless trying. It can be any man who feels entitled to more sex or even just positive attention from women than he can organically procure from them.

It is understandable why the sexless, frustrated male acts as he does—and it is important to at least try to empathize with his pitiful position. He justifies his expectations by the way attractive women make him feel. When he looks upon a woman's pretty face, sexy body, or warm feminine personality, he is infused with unmanageable passion and desire. The incentive to act builds up with nowhere to go. He blames the women who attract him for enchanting him with their femininity and wiles, for instigating impulses that he cannot satisfy on his own and that he does not know how to act on toward them in a fair and ethical manner. He is not ready to recognize that the burden of being a man is his to bear. If he took accountability for his orientation, his romantic and sexual desire would motivate him to improve himself, to become worthy of the comforts and beauty the women he covets can offer.

The incel mindset toward women extends beyond individuals to a societal level. Men in the most primitive, sexually restrictive societies impose their "protection" over nations of women whom they have claimed under their domain because they are co-identified via culture. They force women to behave within certain acceptable confines "for their own good" to limit their power over men. These coercive sexual and relationship beliefs show up most prominently as: "Women from my culture should only date, marry, or have sex with men from my culture because they enforce the correct rules for sexual expression." If women venture outside these bounds, the sexually frustrated men of the culture will interpret it as though they are being deprived of something that is naturally owed to them for being good, upstanding members of their tribe. "If *I* have to live by the limitations of my culture, so do *you*." Such impotent men seek to control women because they fear they will not be able to earn their affection and beauty on their own merit. They know, deep down, that they are not manly enough to be proper men. And because men need this motivation from women so badly, they will seek to contain women to a state where they are almost wholly dedicated to providing it.

If women are property that is automatically owed to men, it means they are not real people with consciousness and individuality they have to discover and become worthy of bonding with. A woman embodying her femininity is wild and uncontrollable in the eyes of such a primitive man. He knows this and fears it...

> *"If we take a survey of ages and of countries, we shall find the women, almost—without exception—at all times and in all places, adored and oppressed. Man, who has never neglected an opportunity of exerting his power, in paying homage to their beauty, has always availed himself of their weakness. He has been at once their tyrant and their slave."*
>
> — Thomas Paine,
> *An Occasional Letter on the Female Sex* (1775)

"PROTECTING" FEMININE PURITY AND INNOCENCE

Under healthy conditions, feminine women are motivating factors for men to become the best masculine men they are capable of being. Good men should be determined to earn the admiration of women organically. Yet, throughout great swaths of the developing world, a term that applies to both culture and economy, we find societies run by men who restrict the freedom and feminine expression of women. What are these chest-beating patriarchs so afraid of? The power they know the feminine form and energy hold over them. It's their kryptonite. The masculine is limited in important emotional aspects that the feminine naturally excels at, so long as a woman is actually allowed to be a woman. Her social restrictions prevent her from doing so except under tightly controlled conditions. One can imagine what a disastrous, inverted world it would be if it were women placing equally harsh regulations on how men are allowed to display their masculinity for fear of the harm it might cause.

In places less barbarous and somewhat more developed, the restrictions men place on women might not be sanctioned as official State policy, but they are still common enough to be expected throughout the culture and enforced through shame, fear, and guilt. Girls are rarely allowed to do nearly as much on their own as boys are. They can't date freely. They can't come home whenever they want. They can't wear whatever they want. They can't express themselves because there is not a real self to express, as it has not been allowed to develop. Marriage is often a social calculation. Parents decide for their children if the pairing is a convenient match for both families. The whole affair seems to have more to do with family politics than love, affection, or chemistry between the bride and groom. It reminds me of the princess from one medieval family being married off to the prince from another to form political and military alliances on a small and pitiful scale. The limitations of parents become the limitations of their sons and daughters, too, in a cyclical burden that no one will break free from until enough men and women are bold enough to recognize it as a form of intergenerational enslavement.

The suppression women endure shows up in many subtle ways beyond the obvious, such as restrictive clothing and unequal rights under the law. One teenage girl I knew practically had a panic attack the first time she contracted vaginal candidiasis, more commonly known as a yeast infection. She was terrified that she had somehow contracted an STD despite not being sexually active. When she finally told her mother about her problem, she refused to let her go to a doctor because doing so would require them to inspect her vagina, which, she falsely believed, could lead to her hymen breaking, thus ruining her sexual market value in a society populated by men obsessed with the perception of feminine "purity." I offered to take her to the doctor myself, but the implication of being seen with an older man under such sensitive conditions was too great an embarrassment to bear. Other women have been afraid to be seen riding in a car with me on the off chance someone sees them and assumes it means they are romantically involved with me, perhaps even on their way to my house to have sex with me right at that moment. Parents may insist that their daughter marry any man she has developed a public association with or else disown her for the shame it might bring. Visiting a man's house alone might as well be equivalent to entering the prostitution profession for them for the social reaction it will incur. The shame often instigates a nervous breakdown and a violent, Gestapo-like reaction from friends and strangers.

These events do not only occur in places where an outsider might already know to expect violent subjugation of women for failing to follow strict social rules. In many places, the cultural suppression of feminine self-expression is enforced with the subtle and devious threat of social ostracism for failing to conform. Girls there know that everyone will shun or hate them if they don't say and do the right things. To them, that's the same as being arrested, beaten, or killed. It's an invisible type of social repression that an outsider might only notice after they've been present long enough to have interacted with the people regularly.

The widespread reaction to the possibility of feminine promiscuity is a terrifying form of social control. Masses of strangers collaborate to spy on potentially unchaste women.

Everyone with eyes is an enemy, an agent willingly participating in the system repressing natural and healthy sexual drives and interests. Big Brother, Big Father, Big Uncle, and Big Future Husband are always watching. Sex education is lacking because if adults were to explain what sex is and how it works in a fair and objective manner, they would risk young people coming to their own conclusions about what an appropriate sex life looks like. The ruling influence would cease to be what one's neighbors might think and what gossip they might spread to bring shame upon one's family.

Around the world, there exist many variations on these dehumanizing ideas regarding the social sanctity of exclusively female virginity. Some sound like they come straight out of the Middle Ages or perhaps from even further back in caveman times. Blood-stained bed sheets might be hung from clotheslines outside the home to brag to the neighborhood that, indeed, the new bride was an unsoiled virgin on her wedding night. Some women who have committed the grievous sin of having a normal sex drive and expressing it before marriage try to restore their dignity in another drastic manner. They might have the hymen surgically reconstructed to hide their shame from their husband, his family, and society at large.

I once assumed that primitive man's obsession with virginity and its loss was related to physical cleanliness and purity. Perhaps such men are overly cautious about the spread of sexually transmitted disease and complete sexual abstinence is the only way to be sure of safety. Or perhaps, for purely psychological reasons, they are uncomfortable sticking their genitals where they know another man has stuck his before. I realized that this couldn't be the case based on the starkly different way that young men in such cultures are often taught to think about sex compared to women. The sanctimonious and exclusive view applied to women is typically the opposite for men. Teenage boys are treated to prostitutes, who might have had hundreds of sexual partners before them, to lose their virginity and become "real men." The same first-time act that is seen as sacred and personal for women is deliberately reduced to its crudest, most animalistic, and impersonal form for men, encouraging the belief that there is something wrong with men for putting intimate value into sex and something wrong with women for not.

For women, the holy status of "virgin" can even extend beyond genital penetration or any form of physical intimacy. Some men won't date women who have had any prior romantic relationships, regardless of how much or how little promiscuity may have been present. Every eligible bachelor in their society would be ashamed of the public association he would carry from not being his girl's first romantic partner. And even after a virginal woman gets married the way she is expected to, she goes on to face ever more restrictions imposed by her new family. The new couple usually goes to live with the groom's parents, where the overbearing mother-in-law will chaperone them for as long as she remains alive and well enough to make demands. There's a tragic irony in this. The mother-in-law acts like the madam of a brothel who oversees the subjugation of younger women. She carries on the tradition of control that she herself was subjected to instead of trying to empower her new daughter-in-law to enjoy freedoms she never could because of the restrictions that were imposed on her when she was young.

Virginity, of course, doesn't actually exist in the way most cultures are conditioned to think about it. It's not a thing you are born with and can lose. It's an anti-concept, like cold or darkness. It's defined only by what it isn't, by the absence of experience of something potentially life-affirming and wonderful. Having sex for the first time is just like doing anything else for the first time—only more physically and emotionally sensitive than most other things we do for the first time.

The Systemic Negation of Feminine Agency

A consequence of viewing men and women as the same kind of being is that women become relegated to classification as undeveloped men. And because of this, men have to care for women who will never progress past immaturity and childishness into adult levels of agency. Many women, unfortunately, accept and celebrate the hobbled gender role passed down to them by men who insist on treating them as beautiful objects and prized possessions. A woman should remain totally naïve and innocent— in every way, a little girl who needs a protective father figure to look over her, except that she is also appropriate for receiving his sexual attention.[13] Because such a woman has little agency of her own, her "choice" to accept a suitor's romantic interest is hardly a choice at all. How could she know any different than to return the affections thrust upon her? How could she even compare him to anyone else? How could she know herself well enough to know what she would prefer if she had freedom and experience? It's why the undeveloped world still prizes female innocence, virginity, and lack of experience. To them, infantile traits are feminine virtues.

In the West, there's been a bit of an overcorrection to this prominent bias against the self-actualization and self-expression of women. Many storytellers have adopted the position that the

---

13 *This understated trope is covered in greater detail in the excellent video essay Born Sexy Yesterday on the YouTube channel Pop Culture Detective: https://www.youtube.com/watch?v=0thpEyEwi80.*

best way to show the strength of a woman is to make her more like a man—faster, stronger, cooler, and with a bigger gun than all the boys. *My Fair Lady*'s Professor Higgins would certainly approve. Are we to believe that this is the peak of feminine power? Women should know they don't need to emulate men to be powerful. Patty Jenkins' *Wonder Woman* is a rare, quality example of a recent feminine heroic arc in popular film. Amazonian Princess Diana undertakes a feminine developmental journey, maturing from a little girl to a grown woman mentally. She begins naïve about the state of the world of man, thinking it perfect and wholly beautiful. She has to discover its ugliness, love it, and choose to spread beauty anyway. Notably, she accomplishes this with the aiding influence of Steve Trevor, an uncommonly good man in the story's chauvinistic World War I setting—not as some kind of contrarian reaction against him or attempt to usurp his masculine role.

None of this is to suggest that women cannot (or should not) display masculine traits, of course. The issue is about *replacing* the feminine variety of strength with the masculine one, often completely overshadowing it and pretending it doesn't even exist. It reaffirms the message that women are weak and immature versions of men, that the only way for a woman to rise above her natural infantile state is to force herself to, well, "be more like a man."

There is a place for a wiser, more experienced man to guide a woman and help her grow so that she will no longer require a teacher, guardian, or mentor. It is not to celebrate and perpetuate her infantility. Quite unexpectedly, James Cameron's *Terminator* duology offers an effective overall meditation on the interplay between masculinity and femininity in an explosive sci-fi action package. Kyle Reese, at first, acts remarkably like the terminator he's meant to stop: a human machine and machine human, respectively. He treats the woman in his life, Sarah Connor, like an objective because that's all she is to him. He's cold and insensitive, just like a machine. Somewhere in the course of interacting with her, he welcomes beauty, love, joy, and an intrinsic reason to protect her beyond the mission assigned to him. Eventually, he shares his vulnerability with her, including the admission that he has been in love with her but unable to express it until then. She, in turn, falls in love with and makes love to him for it. They don't have sex because they're both horny and attractive young people but because they feel a deeper connection to each other than either has ever experienced. Making love to her brings his first true peace and happiness, smiling and relaxing at last. His connection to this woman that he's been helping grow into someone strong and mature compared to the weak little girl she was at the start, someone capable of taking care of herself and defeating killer robots, enables him to become fully human instead of just a soldier on a mission.

> *"I don't belong here. I wasn't meant to see this. It's like a dream. This. And This. And you. It's so beautiful. It hurts, Sarah."*
>
> — Kyle Reese, *The Terminator* (in a deleted scene)

Intelligent but unfeeling machines embody, in ways once technologically impossible, the dangers of conception existing in a vacuum without the capacity for emotional experience—an analogy that is becoming all the more relevant in our increasingly

AI-enabled world. *Terminator 2: Judgment Day* expands on women learning to trust men after having been abused by them, and the focus on the interplay between the masculine and feminine shifts from romantic to parental as Sarah must reluctantly accept that the stubborn traits of masculine strength are necessary in a proper father figure for her son. Sarah, the feminine motivating force from the previous film, now, ironically, embodies the role of cold masculinity. She is the one on a mission where pain, feelings, and beauty don't matter. She displays all the negative effects of a woman trying to *be more like a man.*

Men further infantilize women by making them depend on them socially and economically. Wives are often restricted from taking certain types of jobs or having careers at all because their insecure husbands don't want them to be out of the home for too long. The wife's "job" is to remain at home, tending to the needs of her husband, children, and in-laws. If she were to start earning too much of her own money, it would increase her freedom too much and loosen the overbearing culture's control.

As a young man, I had been told by every reliable source that women were attracted to men with money. But as my income increased, I saw no obvious effects on my dating life because I made few visible changes in my spending habits. I never spent money for the purpose of showing off what I could afford. When I courted a woman at a time when most of my income was spent refurbishing an old homestead, my girlfriend confessed that she was confused by my choice to spend my money in such an unconventional way. "It's very nice. This just isn't how most people spend their money." My naïve partner was making the same mistake golddiggers do by associating wealth with flash instead of substance. It wasn't about having money and the opportunities it brings as a medium of exchange. It was about displaying the willingness to *waste* money on frivolous short-term sources of excitement and social status. Showing off and overspending makes economically limited women feel like a prize to be won.

Every dollar spent on something that brings no long-term, meaningful value to life is a dollar that could have been spent on something that would have accomplished greater good for oneself or the world. It could have been used to acquire education, tools, and resources that would have made you and your partner more capable of expressing yourselves as the people you wish to be. It could have been an investment in the pairing that will define your shared future. What could be more romantic than that?

Men would lose much of their coercive power in the dating and marriage scene if women around the world better understood how to apply their knowledge and skills in economic ways. Exchanging knowledge, skills, and resources for currency is *not* a gendered phenomenon. It is the foundation of mutually beneficial social interaction for all people. Everyone is an entrepreneur[14] seeking to get what they want through their efforts. They can do this via optimized collaboration with others seeking the same or by manipulating others into giving what they believe would be otherwise beyond their reach. Yet, we have accepted and insisted that the role of economic provider is something men are more

---

14 *For a more detailed explanation of how universally true this is, I humbly and unbiasedly recommend you read my book* Everyone Is an Entrepreneur: Selling Economic Self-Determination in a Post-Soviet World *(Identity Publications, 2022).*

capable of than women without justification. Nothing about the natural differences between the sexes makes men fundamentally better at economic exchange, even if women might specialize in different *types* of productivity. But still, women have been indoctrinated into believing that they are economically incapable on their own. Confirmation bias will stop them from processing simple, obvious ways to increase their earning capacity because they have already categorized themselves as non-earners who must depend on a masculine partner to earn *for* them and impress them primarily with *his* material wealth.

Women who seek to be materially spoiled have fallen for the infantilization gambit men love to control them with. They have been told their whole lives that taking care of themselves and being meaningfully productive in the world is beyond them. The alternative they accept is that the greatest good they can do is simply to exist in a largely unconscious, non-participatory role in life, to have all their choices passed down from a higher authority: their breadwinning husband.

In religious cultures, the husband's authority to make conscious choices for the rest of the family (with wife and children usually lumped together into the same incapable category or the wife only marginally above the children) comes from the perception of a masculine deity that holds ultimate conscious authority over everyone. The husband acts as God Daddy's human ambassador for women and children here on Earth, imbued with a small amount of His power to be conscious and choose. To be a good wife is to submit to your husband's will for you and, by extension, his God's.

Submission and passivity are not feminine virtues. Men who seek them in a partner are admitting that they do not see women as fully human, as humanity is defined by the capacity for consciousness and choice. They will try their darndest to keep the women they pursue from realizing everything they are capable of. A secure and actualized woman with an active mind requires so much more to be turned on by a man and seek his complementary partnership. That's not a task most men are up to, and they feel existentially threatened by the mere idea of it. I've received death threats from men who thought I was robbing them of their God-given right to a submissive wife by speaking and writing to empower women in places where they are most culturally subjugated. These are the same men who are intimidated by women who make more money than they do... or who are taller than them, physically stronger than them, more assertive than them, more independent than them, or who have more sexual experience than them. All of these qualities indicate that it will be more difficult for them to exert control over her and fit her into the box they and society have prepared for her.

Non-participation in conscious life is how we interpret the epitome of luxury and lavish recreation: an existence tailored to the immediate nullification of problems to solve and choices to make. A meaningful life is not one devoid of problems but one that embraces a specific order of problems to solve in line with one's deepest values. The most vulnerable women seek an instant solution to the problems inherent to consciously participating in life. They are attracted to men of means because they see them as easy "off" buttons to the struggles of daily life.

They learn early on that if they are submissive and sexy enough, the right man, a veritable Prince Charming, will ride in on a white horse and spare them from a life of toil. It's the opposite of a mature man who seeks a woman who will *enliven* him with her motivating influence. She helps him become *more* of himself, just as he does the same for her. He does not seek to nullify her identity. The promise of false security is a permanent state of non-action while the world turns around you without you as a conscious participant. It is spiritual suicide for women.

In sum: Women have been treated as not fully human by men, as not fully conscious and autonomous beings deserving of their own identity, volition, and freedom to express their authentic selves. They are classified as glorified pets if they are lucky and as slaves if they are not. The trophy wife is the pinnacle of what a woman under such coercive control can aspire to: having an owner who takes good care of her and benevolently compensates her for her beauty and subservience.

CHAPTER 3

Attraction, Meaningful and Superficial

> *"What imperative does a gray box have to interact with another gray box?"*
>
> — Nathan Bateman, *Ex Machina*

For the immature, undeveloped man, physical beauty seems to be the dominant romantic drive, if not the exclusive one. The mere observation of what he considers an attractive woman instigates a series of thoughts and emotions that impel him to try to talk to her, maybe get her phone number, take her on a date, or bring her back home for a chance to see her naked over the course of days, weeks, months, or even years. That's an awful lot of work to commit to, all initially motivated by an appealing feminine sight that cannot be ignored until acted on.

That you are physically attracted to a woman, even a complete stranger, is a very easy conclusion to arrive at. And there's nothing inherently wrong with it. Finding a woman attractive (and even sleeping with her just for the visceral experience of it) is not unhealthy, immature, or immoral, so long as no one is being manipulated or expecting more from the encounter than it can offer. It's *easy* to look attractive to men, which is what makes undeveloped women preoccupied with the task instead of focusing on building fundamentally attractive *character*. Superficial women exploit that men are wired to notice them because it's much easier than building deeper, sustainable attraction based on *all* types of chemistry beyond the physical. You could have amazing psychological chemistry with someone, but you're not going to figure that out as instantaneously as you figure out that you think they look nice. If a woman thinks her primary asset is her looks, she'll be much less likely to prioritize the development of her character and everything else that makes deep romantic bonding possible.

Personally, I've always been fascinated by how easily I can tell if I am attracted to a woman, even at a great distance or in a low-resolution photo. My brain instantly highlights her for me and signals, "Hey, there's one. You should look into her more. Maybe go start a conversation. She passes." It's some combination of her body shape, skin tone, and facial features that I am scarcely aware of on a conscious level. But the reactions are always there. Most men could probably spot a woman they are physically attracted to from a mile away out of the corner of their eye.

Instant visual attraction of this kind is a good motivator to start talking to someone—a doorway, of sorts, to potentially something more. But for a deep romantic bond to form, it cannot be enough merely for a woman to be physically attractive to a man. It should not even be noteworthy, no more so than any other shiny object that might momentarily capture your attention only to immediately be forgotten. A mature man seeks that in a partner that is most deeply and fundamentally attractive to him. Do you even understand yourself well enough to know what that is?

Romantic attraction requires extreme discrimination. Otherwise, you will get excited about and pine after every new woman who enters your life under vaguely positive circumstances or who looks tempting in a sundress. Romantic vision is tunnel vision. There has to be something extraordinary about this person in your eyes that sets them above and apart from the rest of humanity—one bright shining star in a sea of darkness and mediocrity. Romantic interest is extreme specialization: depth, not breadth.

But because feminine visual appeal is so much easier to achieve than any other kind, we are stuck in a horrible situation where women are encouraged to look as hot or beautiful as possible to earn attention from men because it's socially valuable. Pornography, celebrity culture, and social media condition us to focus on how a woman looks, on how visually sexy and superstimulating[15] she is. Men are so inundated with this cheap attraction that they can't begin to focus on what really matters to them, what qualities they would find far more rewarding in a woman beyond the curves of her body (not that there's anything wrong with the love of a good curve). It's a vicious, superficial cycle. A supervicious cycle.

Just because a woman is physically attractive doesn't mean it has to *mean* something. Sometimes, it just means that a woman is physically attractive. A smoother pebble or prettier shell than

---

15 *A superstimulus is anything that stimulates a normally positive or useful response so highly that it becomes detrimental, well past its original, useful parameters, including indicators of sexual attraction. For instance, in Supernormal Stimuli (W. W. Norton & Company, 2010), evolutionary psychologist Deirdre Barrett describes an orchid that mimics heightened characteristics of a female wasp's torso to incentivize male wasps to ejaculate on it and spread pollen, even though there is no possibility of the wasp achieving its goal of reproduction. There is a similar human male tendency to be brought to arousal and ejaculation by the mere image of a feminine form with exaggerated sexual features.*

the rest is just a smooth pebble or pretty shell—unless you obsess and make it mean something more than it should. There has to be a part of you that is as excited by the holistic principle of a woman as you are by how good she looks naked. *That's* romance. I hope that mature women know to fall for men for whom their existence (*including* their appearance) stimulates latent masculine emotional capacity and makes the world come alive. It's integral and integrative. Anything else is infatuation or its horny cousin lust.

Of course, all other things being equal, you would prefer a partner you find visually appealing to one you don't. But that's another point. It's about what *you* find visually appealing. And it's certainly not about who would be the most coveted piece of arm candy you could parade around in public. Would your eyes be so drawn to porn stars and lingerie models if you were not inundated by a culture that puts them everywhere and tells you they are the women you should be trying to woo? Do you even know what physical features you find most appealing in a woman? The answer might be different from the prevailing answers in your culture. Do you even remember what women look like beneath the charade of makeup, hairstyles, and other masks they have been influenced to wear for your benefit?

ROMANTIC CHEMISTRY BEYOND THE PHYSICAL

I don't believe in love at first sight. There's just not enough you can know by looking at someone, being near them, or briefly talking to them to draw the conclusion that you are in love with them, no matter how they might make the blood pump to your brain or other organs. Regardless, I know from personal experience that you *can* recognize love compatibility and high levels of romantic chemistry with the right person almost as soon as you meet them

—what the Japanese call koi no yokan, or a premonition that you will eventually fall in love with someone. You can definitely see the potential in someone new if you are experienced in this domain and know your authentic preferences well. Under these conditions, you're not just excited because it's a new person and they're so pretty or so interesting. You get a sense that you are aligned on many levels, from the superficial to the super deep. And at the end of a first date or meet-cute,[16] you have a hard time picturing anything you would have had happen differently than it did. And unless either of you employed deception to create an embellished appearance, things might just start to unfold exactly as that marvelous first encounter made you think they would.

Romantic chemistry is a measure of how well someone's existence complements your own in all regards, as much as humanly possible, and yours theirs. It comes in many forms, well beyond the obvious. And when there is enough of it, you get a quick sense that, somehow, you have already known this person much longer than you actually have—like your brain inferred their existence long before you ever met them because it had to believe that someone like them, someone so complementary to you existed somewhere out there in the world. It almost feels like you are remembering each other rather than getting to know each other for the first time—like they are someone you already walked with once upon a dream.

Physical chemistry is when my body feels drawn to yours. It feels good around yours. It can be overt sexual excitement and also just a general sense of comfort in your proximity. When I touch you. When I smell you. When I look at you. I am locked

---

16 *A meet-cute is a first memorable incidental encounter between people who eventually become romantically involved as a consequence of their charming start.*

into the pure experience of your physical form. That is holistic physical beauty and attraction—not the compartmentalized variety that cuts a woman up into attractive pieces to fixate on for the rush they induce. It helps reduce the effects of stress and conflict that inevitably come up in any relationship because I am quickly reminded of how good you make me feel just by existing in my life.

It's how a woman becomes the most beautiful woman in the world to me. It's not that I look around the room and immediately rate her as more visually appealing than anyone I've ever known. She has to have the base capacity for it from the start, certainly. But it's only over the course of learning with her, studying her face and every part of her body, or smelling her and running my hands all over her that she becomes the most attractive woman I've ever seen from that base potential of physical chemistry between us.

Poor physical chemistry could be as obvious as, "I look at you, and it doesn't make me happy. The sight of you doesn't instantly draw me to you. Or worse, it even repels me." It could be that they smell funny to you. Those indicators are easy to recognize. But it could also be something that takes longer to notice. Someone might look quite attractive to you but your bodies don't fit the way they should. You don't know how to move together and touch each other right. The push and pull always feels off. Your bodies don't communicate well, and no matter how hard you try to work on it, progress in this domain might continue to elude the two of you.

Good physical chemistry can be so powerful between two people that it overcomes almost all other barriers to bonding and communication. I've had prolonged, mutually rewarding sexual relationships with women I could barely even speak the same language as, making it impossible for us to verbally share deep, personal truths about each other and assess the ways in which we might be compatible. But what was clear was that our bodies were drawn together and we fed well off of each other's non-verbal cues about how to touch and navigate around each other. There's something very zen about it, which can heighten intimacy. You mostly just experience this person's presence as they are, right there in front of you. And they do the same with you, as you are, right there in front of them. There's little narrative you learn about each other to affect your perception or interaction.

Psychological chemistry is when I talk to you, and the thoughts from your brain complement mine. That's why soulmates can talk for hours and hours about almost anything. It's like each one is interacting with a mind that is an extension of itself. Each partner's mind alone can't go as readily to all the places it does when they are conjoined in conversation, but it feels completely natural when they go there together. They are separate parts of the same machine working together toward the same goal. That's a pretty good way to describe sex, too, come to think of it.

Emotional chemistry is when you can make me feel the things that I can't easily feel on my own, such as peace, joy, beauty, and all those soft virtues that elude the masculine mind operating on its own. A feminine woman might feel more cared for, secure, brave, and maybe even worshiped and honored when she interacts with a man with whom she has considerable emotional chemistry. Everyone with a healthy mind, of course, has the capacity to feel the full spectrum of human emotions, but they are limited and skewed when operating alone. There will always be some areas where they naturally excel more than others. Chemistry, as the name implies, creates new reactions in both of them.

A woman I was in the process of falling in love with didn't believe me when I told her that I had the temperament of a grumpy old man most of the time. She said I was always so happy, that I was always so playful and energetic around her. I told her that was a great example of a selection bias, not a fair overall sampling of my behavior. She only ever saw how I was when I was around her, which was markedly different than when I *wasn't* around her. Our natural emotional chemistry brought out the parts of me that were absent in almost every other category of experience for me. I did the same for her. She added color to my overwhelmingly gray world and couldn't see what a powerful sign of our compatibility that was.

Intellectual chemistry doesn't mean similar levels of education or IQ. It means similar attitudes toward thinking and learning. The woman who ends up with me has to love to learn because I do. She doesn't have to have a bachelor's or master's degree or PhD. She just has to be constantly growing in her ability to think about the world because that's an essential part of my life and identity. If I were constantly learning without her, I would quickly outpace her mentally, and it would become very difficult to continue bonding with her on the same level. There will always be things I know more about than her and things she knows more about than me. Sharing our knowledge and specializations is part of our partnership.

Lifestyle chemistry is when our lifestyle choices complement each other's, which is another way of saying that we have a similar way of navigating the world and pursuing what we want in society. A lifestyle can take on an infinite number of forms. In principle, we have to be aligned. Chemistry is when our wants in this regard are similar enough that there can be a consensus about how we will live instead of merely a series of compromises between us. We have to be willing to work out the details of how to bring our separate lifestyles together as one, such as our professions and income, our family and friends, and where and how we want to live in harmony with one another so that we can function as a bonded unit.

Incidentally, this is one reason men have often subjugated the women of their cultures and insisted on bonding with them while they are still young and dependent. They don't want them to develop their own personalities and lifestyles that could clash with what their husbands would choose for them. Good pets must be trained well according to the preferences of their owners.

Cultural chemistry is misleading because it has nothing to do with the real people underneath their inherited cultural identities. Yet, it is given the greatest weight by people who have not developed their individuality and grown consciously strong enough to assert their own choices. This is something you gain a particularly deep appreciation for the more you travel and the more cultures you are directly exposed to.

Love is all about two people bonding over who they really are. So, whatever culture someone else starts from might seem to be a limitation if it's radically different from your own. The two of you might not expect all the unexamined aspects of reality to work the same way at the start of your partnership. You might not have grown up watching the same movies, listening to the same music, or eating the same food, so you don't have all the same automatic referents. Love is about overcoming those limitations through learning about one another because you are so irresistibly drawn to the person you see underneath all those details.

A shared cultural identity among lovers becomes, at best, a convenience to self-aware people. Together, you replace shared unconscious expectations with shared conscious understanding.

You make choices you would not have known to make on your own (but that ultimately serve you) because of your cultural discrepancies, if for no other reason than to learn about the other person's influences and way of seeing the world. Isn't it so interesting (not threatening) that it differs from your own in so many unexpected ways? Isn't it great that you have the opportunity to introduce them to so many valuable things you mostly take for granted about your worldview? It prevents both of you from being locked into a narrow range of cultural comfort your whole life and passing on those same comfort limits to your children.

In all regards, romantic chemistry is a matter of two people becoming as fully self-expressed as they can on their own, then reaching a whole new, much higher and deeper level of shared expression as a result of bonding and identifying with each other. Your culture is just what you know about yourself so far, what the world has so far *allowed* you to know about yourself. Romantic love should give you all the incentive in the world to learn the rest through the lens of a miraculously complementary partner. With enough time, patience, determination, and all other forms of chemistry aligning, there are no cultural limitations between two compatible and willing lovers that cannot be overcome.

That's what most great love stories are about, after all: coming together in spite of all the cultural pressures to stay apart— forbidden love succeeding at all costs between people who, somehow, feel like they already know each other.

It's hard to appreciate how misleading attraction based wholly on the physical can be unless you've been on the receiving end of it, which isn't a common experience for most men. Most women are not nearly as visually oriented in this regard, and they have much higher standards for what they consider physically attractive enough to send them into a state of active romantic desire without any other qualifying factors.

Aesthetic standards differ across cultures. What is plain and unremarkable in one place is noteworthy or unignorable in another. I've lived in parts of the world where I suddenly found myself turning the heads of local women in public. I was an anomaly in their environment. They compared me to American movie stars, who, of course, I bore little actual resemblance to. Though this new level of attention was flattering and exhilarating at first, I quickly came to see how superficial it was. Sure, it had its uses. I was given special treatment in many situations, and it was relatively easy to find women to take on dates or even sleep with. I suppose this is the typical "hot girl" treatment that women who put excessive attention into their looks are accustomed to receiving. Being considered inordinately attractive grants you "pretty privilege" and lets you play the social game you might normally struggle with on easy mode. Strangers are eager to talk to you, help you out with anything, and go out of their way to make your life as convenient as possible. It's like you are a minor celebrity everywhere you go. It explains why so many women are terrified of losing their looks as they get older. This privilege of an attractive social aura is all they've ever known.

An automatic positive sexual reaction from virile young women sounds like a dream come true for many men. It's the highest, often most unattainable goal for them. Legions of books and videos are dedicated to learning to overcome this obstacle and earn smidgens of attention from beautiful women. But after a while, the cheeky attention women would give me as what they perceived as an extraordinarily handsome man became more irritating than convenient. Once the novelty wore off, I just wanted to be talked to like a person again without any special emotional overlay.

Not all attention is equal. You can't bond with someone over how pretty or sexy they look. The same applies to how interesting they are. An interesting man grabs the attention of a woman just as quickly and superficially as a sexy woman grabs the attention of a man. When a man primarily wants to keep a woman around because she is beautiful or sexy, it is because he needs an object to stimulate him or get his rocks off to. He does not treat her as a living, conscious vessel. A dull woman, likewise, is looking to fill a lack of entertainment in her life with a man, just as the bitter and beautyless man is looking to fill a void in his. She sees him as an amusement, not a person to bond with.

Too many times, I found myself in faulty relationships with women who were drawn to me because they found me more interesting than any other man in their lives. They used me to make themselves more interesting. The real nature of our relationship only became apparent when I tried to move things to a more intimate level and found they lacked the capacity or desire for anything more than the current role I was playing for them. In the worst of cases, I have flown great distances to faraway countries to meet women I had been getting to know for months online. As soon as I arrived, I was treated like a stranger. These women were now forced to confront the reality of their interesting internet boyfriend, who, up until that point, had only lived in a video frame or chat box on their computers. There were no consequences for the expectations they set so long as they did not have to consider me as a flesh-and-blood human being. They dehumanized me in much the same way that immature men everywhere dehumanize the attractive women they see as beautiful objects. Gregory: the interesting object.

I do not cultivate the appearance of an interesting man for the purpose of wooing women, though there are certainly many men who do this. "Be mysterious and interesting" is among the most common pieces of advice given by professional pickup artists who train hopeless men in the art of convincing women to date or sleep with them. They know its power. They are equivalent to women who overload on makeup, clothes, and accessories that are meant to make them look sexually enticing to men. Both are playing manipulation games for personal gain at the expense of another person's disappointed expectations.

Intrigue, like beauty, is not a bad quality in itself. In an ideal social environment, women would be celebrated for being beautiful, men would be celebrated for being interesting, and all people would have an ideal position in society to let all their various character virtues shine through. The essential difference between that hypothetical world and ours is the element of social manipulation. Women who cultivate beauty for the sake of manipulating men are perpetuating harm on them in the long run, just as are men who cultivate intrigue for the purpose of manipulating women.

The conundrum, then, is how a naturally sexy or beautiful woman and a naturally interesting man can display these qualities without attracting the wrong kind of attention. We must recognize these qualities for what they are: ways to get our attention. They are great incentivizers and conversation starters. They cannot be the basis for sustained, meaningful interaction between men and women. You love a man or woman, ultimately, for their character and your unique chemistry with them. When you love someone, you love them under all possible conditions through which they might one day express themselves, not just the ideal ones they've tailored for your present entertainment.

BEAUTIFUL OBJECT SYNDROME[17]

Many women learn very early on that life is a lot easier if they dress or act a certain way to appease a general audience of men. Strangers become more friendly, helpful, doting, and subservient in the presence of feminine beauty. And when they realize this, many of these poor, sexy souls stop developing in every other way that matters because there is no social imperative to. Once they get used to playing the social game on easy mode, it's quite difficult to willfully give that up and choose to make life harder than it has to be.

An attractive young woman has less incentive to develop things like character, knowledge, and skill, including even how to treat other people with respect. Less attractive people require such qualities to survive and function in society because they do not receive automatic prestige and acceptance for the pleasing aura they emit. Women who have always been attractive probably think that's just how life is. If they ever lose that, they might have to start to play the social game that has always been easy on the hardest difficulty with everyone else. And they will quickly realize they have no idea how to win on their own merit.

Appearing attractive isn't even worth as much as it used to be because it's not so rare anymore. Virtually every young woman can make herself up to catch masculine attention if she is inclined. Any such woman who dedicates time to being universally attractive is communicating something about how she sees herself and what her priorities are. There is an entire trope[18]

---

17 *Inspired by a satirical article from The Onion, Teenage Girl Blossoming Into Beautiful Object: https://www.theonion.com/teenage-girl-blossoming-into-beautiful-object-1819574448.*

18 *Look to Sabrina, My Fair Lady, Grease, Never Been Kissed, She's All That, The Princess Diaries, The Devil Wears Prada, and countless others for culturally relevant ugly duckling examples in film.*

dedicated to the phenomenon of a proverbial ugly duckling (i.e., a conventionally unattractive woman), who elevates herself into a position of higher social standing by conforming to general beauty standards—usually at the expense of her authentic personality, hobbies, and values (and hopefully having learned a valuable lesson by the end). Now, whenever I see a woman who has put a lot of work into her appearance, I wonder what she has had to sacrifice and how she is socially rewarded for her effort. I wonder if the trade-off is worth it for her.

An experienced man should know that appearance is not an indicator of character, personality, or meaningful social value. It's imperative for distracted young men to grow past the stage of having their brains taken over by the sight of feminine beauty. That impulse that impels us to try to earn the favor of women simply because they look a certain way cannot rule us. Ask yourself if you would still be talking to such a woman, trying to earn her attention, if she were not pretty or sexually enticing. Picture every physical change she is likely to undergo in time. Is this woman going to remain the most beautiful woman in the world to you in the decades to come? Even if these changes are nothing more than the natural process of aging, as her face develops wrinkles and previously tight parts of her body loosen here and there? Will you still recognize, love, and worship the principle of who she is?

It's easy to be attracted to a woman when she is 20 and still meeting the youth-centric norms of beauty based on health and fertility, such as when her breasts are perky, her skin is tight, and her figure cuts an enticing silhouette. When you look at women in their thirties, forties, fifties, and beyond, the rate of them instigating immediate attraction to the common male suitor falls. What explains this? These men were not attracted to the principle of the women who caught their attention, only their temporarily embellished sensual qualities. That's the danger of falling in love with a young woman—it's easy to delude yourself due to how heightened your sexual response to her is while she is in this temporary state. You are not loving the principle of everything she is and will become.

Appropriately, that's one of the benefits of having had intimate experiences with women at many stages of life, both those younger and older than you. You gain a deeper understanding of how women's bodies and how they display their sensuality evolve with time. You stop expecting every woman to keep desperately clinging to her vibrant, nubile self. She becomes less ambiguously attractive to *all* men and increases the depth of her attractiveness to a specific type of man who is more holistically drawn to her. That's the kind of man she should be wise enough to partner with out of all the horny options that proposition her when she is most outwardly attractive. Men have the inverse problem to worry about: attaching themselves to a woman who, it turns out, was not an inherent match for them but only temporarily overwhelming with her beauty. This is the world we live in, a world of primitive sexual impulses ramped up to 11 and made the foundation of social identity.

An immature man, when he looks upon a woman with lust or sexual passion in his heart (and other organs), has the unfortunate tendency of reducing her to a non-volitional object for satisfying his carnal needs. In the worst case, a woman exposed to a culture of this from the time she is born accepts her role in this process. It becomes the primary source of her social value. She no longer knows who she is without it, which explains why so many aging women are terrified of who they might become to the world once their physical beauty starts to fade. They have scarcely little identity without it.

What does feminine beauty offer a man besides a momentary hit of endorphins? We don't have to deny the pleasant distraction it provides by pretending it isn't there or turning away like self-denying monks. We just have to realize that finding a woman physically attractive is not much of an accomplishment by itself. It will happen hundreds of times a day if we let it. We shouldn't confuse instant physical attraction for anything substantial.

Once a woman has become primarily identified with her visual appeal, it is easy to overlook all her other capacities and even for her to permanently fail to develop them. She might forget she even has them because she sees no social value compared to the instant reward she receives for being hot, cute, sexy, pretty, or beautiful. Men, too, forget that there was once a persona under there, one they would treat no differently than any stranger walking down the street if she didn't happen to inhabit a shell that automatically incites certain chemical reactions in their caveman brains, initiating but not fulfilling the mating process in their bodies.

> *"Youth and beauty are not accomplishments. They're temporary, happy by-products of time and/or DNA. Don't hold your breath for either."*
>
> — Carrie Fisher

I am glad that I now have the composure to see a drop-dead gorgeous woman as both a divine aesthetic experience *and* a conscious agent worthy of my respect. Men, when you see a hot woman, acknowledge it and move on with your life.

OKAY, SO YOU'RE AN INSTAGRAM MODEL? THAT DON'T IMPRESS-A-ME MUCH[19]

My generation, Millennials, was the last to grow up without social media to publicly document our embarrassing youthful behavior. The same behaviors that people my age and older are ashamed to look back on about themselves are what young people today are deliberately showing off and trying to get internet clout for. Time will tell if this might contribute to a permanent state of arrested development for them. It's a new type of social neoteny.[20] We reward infantile behavior, creating incentives not to develop past psychological infancy.

I am frequently in shock and awe at how much content is produced, shared, and adored that seems to have little more reason to exist than a cheap opportunity to look at a woman's face, legs, groin, midriff, breasts, or ass. I wonder if the teen girls being influenced by the viral trends of the day will realize they are participating in simulated sexual behavior to arouse and entice legions of creepy older men. It's a modern, technologically enabled, and socially rewarded take on the world's oldest profession. An exceptional few of these economically motivated beautiful objects

---

19 *Note for future generations: This heading contains two cultural references that might become unrecognizable in the years to come. The first is the concept of an "Instagram model." Instagram is a photo-sharing social media platform started in 2010 that came to be predominantly populated by "influencers" who indulged in vanity by posting vapid photos of themselves for clout. The second is the 1997 Shania Twain song That Don't Impress Me Much. The chorus consists of Shania listing common superficial traits about men that, as the title suggests, fail to impress her much.*

20 *"Neoteny" is a term from evolutionary biology that refers to the retention of juvenile or immature traits in adulthood because they provide survival or procreative benefits, seen everywhere in nature but most notably in humans and their domesticated animals. It can include both physical traits (such as sparse body hair, big eyes, and virtually anything we consider "cute" that instigates a caretaking instinct) and personality traits (such as playfulness, helplessness, and docility).*

ascend the hierarchy of social value as professional models, influencers, and other mediums of beautiful-objectry, wherein they contribute virtually nothing to the world beyond their fetishized appearance for as many years as they are blessed with obvious visual indicators of peak nubile fertility.

In 2007, when I was a senior in high school at San Dieguito Academy in North San Diego County, there was a popular girl two years below me, widely known as the archetypal "hot girl." She was the daughter of the school's art teacher and was locally famous for her developed physical assets and captivating appearance at such a young age. She and I shared many mutual friends and were even chosen to co-host some school events together because we were both well-known around the school.[21] One of my male classmates approached me after one such event and uttered, "Man, that girl's so hot," as if to congratulate me for the good fortune of having been in her presence and publicly associated with her. Already, at 18, I was annoyed with the idea of women being reduced to their looks, so I responded, "What girl?" feigning that I had no idea who he could possibly be referring to with such a callous description and walked away from this now visibly confused young man.

From time to time in the years following high school, I would still see something about the hot girl show up in my social media timeline shared by our mutual friends. It seemed that she was getting into modeling. I would start to see professional photos of her in bikinis and lingerie posted by the people we both knew. Then, one day—I don't recall exactly when—I realized I was seeing pictures of her posted not by any mutual friends but

---

21 *My school notoriety was for very different reasons, though, such as living out of a van during senior year and, eventually, getting kicked out of school for refusing to wear shoes to class... but that's a story for another book.*

by popular entertainment websites like *Sports Illustrated*. And suddenly, she was in a nude scene in a movie as Ben Affleck's young mistress and parading her uncensored tits around in some controversial R&B music video. The hot girl from my high school was supermodel Emily Ratajkowski, now world-famous for the coveted superstimulating combination of a slim figure and full breasts.

It's odd to have memories of the teenage popular chick version of Emily. I have witnessed her grow into what is, so far as I can tell from a distance, a hyperbolic version of the social identity she had back then, now with skeezy horndog men around the world going gaga and writing lewd public comments about what they want to do to her. A significant portion of her public brand identity now exists as masturbatory fuel for the lowliest, least worthy-of-respect modern cavemen on the planet—which some interpret as empowering for women, many of whom still have little freedom over how they express their sexual agency. It's a bit surreal, even. I cannot escape seeing naked or nearly naked images of the most popular girl from my high school. She has transitioned into a beautiful object for the world at large and is richly compensated for it. She is the success story that young women who reduce themselves to being superficially attractive for clout can only dream of. It's the apex of social value that can come from walking this path and embracing this social identity.

I don't do much to intentionally keep up with Emily's career developments except out of mild curiosity about a culturally notable figure I was acquainted with long ago. Still, I can't help but feel a bit sympathetic toward her despite her career accomplishments. Her attitude of feminine sexual empowerment is, at times, betrayed by comments that reveal how she, one of the most sexually desired women in the world (and, by corollary, one of the most powerful), remains just as insecure as every common girl seeking validation with ungodly amounts of makeup, showy attire, and flattering poses for the sake of winning strangers' approval online.

> *"I post Instagram photos that I think of as testaments to my beauty and then obsessively check the likes to see if the internet agrees. I collect this data more than I want to admit, trying to measure my allure as objectively and brutally as possible. I want to calculate my beauty to protect myself, to understand exactly how much power and lovability I have."*
>
> — Emily Ratajkowski, *My Body*
> (Metropolitan Books, 2022)

From this perspective, the woman with the body and lifestyle that so many millions of others insecurely compare themselves to comes across as weak, like she's dependent on the opinions of others for her sense of self. Yet, despite her self-aware admission that it's a shallow pursuit, Emily continues to show off her body online to her tens of millions of followers.[22] Common women can learn something from this brave confession. Even if you ascend to the top of the social-sexual hierarchy and acquire all the power and attention that comes with it, you will probably still feel inadequate. There must be a better path to self-worth for the self-aware woman.

---

22 *To be fair, if I could make millions of dollars by removing my clothes and posting a few selfies on the internet, I'd probably do it, too. But I certainly wouldn't have my sense of identity or self-worth wrapped up in it.*

I encourage young women who idolize gorgeous models and actresses to consider how, even for them, there is no end to the self-serving pursuit of social praise as a beautiful object. And it's a losing battle. You can't beat entropy forever. The issue will only get worse as you get older. If someone like Emily Ratajkowski is brave and self-aware enough to admit that she is trapped in a cycle of appealing to the crowd for validation, what hope does the average teenage girl debasing herself for social media praise have of seeing through the ruse and focusing on developing genuine character instead? Until Emily and the millions like her can separate their sense of identity from the social reaction to their beauty, they will remain slaves to the least qualified masculine masters: the crude men who give them this power with their primitive sexual reactions.

As a man, I cannot imagine having my sense of self-worth so tied up in the world's expectations of me. It sounds utterly exhausting. Similarly, I can no longer imagine evaluating any of these poor women's entire social worth by how they look in photos or videos online. To paraphrase a very wise woman: Looking good naked simply doesn't impress me much.

MARRY THE WOMAN WHO IS MOST ATTRACTIVE WHEN SHE'S LEAST ATTRACTIVE

Hardly a heterosexual man on Earth would deny that the body parts famous supermodels regularly show off are pleasant to look at. They have optimized for universal sexual appeal and earned various degrees of fame and riches because of it. But someone like them could never come close to how intensely I feel when I look at just the right woman for me, no matter what the rest of the world thinks of her.

I'm intrigued by what features I find myself consistently attracted to. Like most men, I definitely have a "type"—certain physical features that show up frequently in the women I'm most attracted to, which can be completely different than what most of the men I associate with will say they are most attracted to. Among these features are dark hair, large facial features, and smooth skin. She is usually a bit shorter than me and lean, but not with an overly skinny or muscled frame. Breasts on the smallish side, proportional to her frame. A look of wit and determination to her, like you can just sense how much she has to say about something. Most men could probably describe the general set of traits they find most attractive in women without having to think too hard about it, even if they've never explicitly thought about it in those terms.

Yet, there is also a variety of physical features outside these parameters that will entice me in unique ways. Bigger breasts or flatter chests. Lighter or darker skin tones and hair colors. Different body shapes and sizes. Part of me wants to experience them all at least a little. The novelty adds to it, even if she isn't the most attractive woman in the world to me or the woman I would want to take to bed every night and wake up next to every morning. There's a latent sexual curiosity in me that perks up when I am exposed to sexual novelty, though it is not nearly as strong now in my mid-thirties as it was when I was younger and it chronically hijacked my attention. As well, I can easily grow more attracted to someone who didn't happen to match all my automatic preferences in physicality if chemistry in other domains is strong enough.

I often think about the primordial evolutionary impulse that might be responsible for creating my overwhelming interest in sexual novelty. Why do men so often want a chance to see so many women naked at least once? Why do men so quickly move on to the next target after fucking a woman one time? Why does the archetype of the pickup artist, player, or fuckboy[23] exist? And why do we praise men for having convinced many women to sleep with them? Perhaps men are made to want to spread their seed far and wide, under as many genetic conditions as possible for the greatest chance at viable offspring.

Many men are eager to sleep with anything even remotely feminine and willing to get naked around them. They hardly discriminate at all. Further, I am frequently confused and/or disgusted by what other men uphold as the peak of sexiness. Just go to any popular pornography website and browse the "highest rated" or "most viewed" categories to get a too-intimate look at what degrading horrors get the common man off most often—which seem to almost exclusively concentrate on acts and angles that emphasize the relegation of women and their bodies to non-volitional objects for men's bestial fetishism. Perhaps the common disempowered man gets off to a superficial sense of power over women because he feels so powerless to attract them in real life.

Some of my most intimate sexual experiences have been with women I wasn't particularly physically attracted to, who didn't fit my default mold for overwhelming sexiness or beauty. Not that there was anything wrong with them—they just weren't

---

23 *The term "fuckboy" describes a man who manipulates women into sleeping with him by talking and acting the way he knows they want him to. His explicit goal is cheap, transactional sex with women under the guise of wanting something more.*

who I would have picked out from a crowd at first glance. But our communication and our shared goals, all our other types of chemistry, were so strong that we were able to craft a meaningful sexual experience together. A base level of physical compatibility and comfort was enough to unlock some of the benefits of deeper physical intimacy.

To a sexually oriented and empowered man, every remotely attractive woman is a sexual option. That doesn't mean he plans on seducing every single one of them—who has the time for that? It doesn't mean he can't be genuine friends with a pretty girl without some ulterior plot to get her into bed or that he can't appreciate all the other forms of value she embodies beyond her sexual appeal. It just means he sees sex in a category not too distinct from most other categories of social interaction: the natural outcome of two mutually attracted people moving progressively closer to one another.

You like what you like, and there's no getting around that. It is just as hard to imagine pair-bonding with someone you hold a great deal of psychological affinity for but are physically repulsed by as it is with someone you are physically drawn to but with whom you have no common values. I would even go so far as to say that infatuation and, to a degree, lust are necessary components of healthy romantic love and bonding. You have to want to look at and be around your partner. You have to want to touch them, to merge with and mold into them, both physically and emotionally. It's an essential part of romantic bonding, with sexual intercourse itself being the culmination of this process.

Genuine physical chemistry probably also reveals important aspects of natural genetic and biochemical compatibility between partners—but I'm no biologist, so don't ask me.

Greatly complicating the matter is that modern man has been spoiled and, to a large extent, corrupted by constant exposure to manufactured feminine attractiveness. We are reared into a world of sexual superstimulation that overwhelms our senses by giving us more of a good thing than would be naturally possible. It's the high-fructose corn syrup of sexual aesthetics. We don't know how to process it all. As such, we are oversexed and underfucked: infused with powerful motivators we haven't learned how best to act on. Modern artificialities create the possibility that you might not even know what the woman you see every day actually looks like—only the mask and tailored persona she adopts before she leaves the house each morning. You might not know how attracted to her you really are. You might only know the image she has crafted, which she probably picked up from generalized beauty standards in her local culture. In the worst cases, she will surgically alter herself to look less and less like herself and more and more how men like you have told her she ought to. Is she making these drastic changes just "for herself," as so many women will claim? Or because she has been inundated with cultural ideas about what it means to be beautiful and socially valued? Think about why "the red dress"[24] and its counterpart, "the little black dress," exist as motifs in women's fashion. What purpose do they serve? What social response does

---

24 *Morpheus in* The Matrix *warned us of the consciousness-hijacking potential of feminine beauty during the scene involving the woman in the red dress who suddenly turns out to be a deadly agent of the matrix in disguise: "Were you listening to me, Neo? Or were you looking at the woman in the red dress? Look again."*

the woman who dons them anticipate by doing so? They are tools for a purpose: to capture attention and use it.

Makeup and clothing don't have to be deceptive or inauthentic, of course. Most of the time, when I see someone wearing everyday clothes, it does little to influence my perception of what that person looks like. On both conscious and unconscious levels, I register that your baggy sweatshirt is just some cloth you draped over your body to keep it warm and covered. Even a dress shirt and jacket are just context-specific cultural costumes. But often, when women manufacture their appearance through expertly crafted adornments and decorations, they are engaging in social manipulation. They cease to look like themselves because they want to fit a standard that the world will find generally pleasing. It's socially advantageous for them. They are simultaneously victims of and the perpetrators behind an increasingly unreal social world.

Beauty is as attractive as vanity is unattractive, which is ironic because the more beautiful you are, the more vain you are likely to be. Is there anything less attractive than an attractive man or woman who knows how attractive they are? True beauty requires a degree of humility. It is not something consciously sought after and meticulously manicured into being. Vanity is the opposite. It's awareness of and obsession with appearing as attractive as possible, even cultivating attraction for the purpose of social manipulation. The woman who is beautiful without explicitly trying to be beautiful is the most beautiful of all. The most attractive woman in the world is usually the one who does not quite realize how attractive she is or who is attractive in a specific way to a specific type of man—a man who will value her above all other women and not have every man in the world competing for her attention. Such a woman will not have made universal visual appeal the foundation of who she is in the world.

I fell in love with a woman who looked about five times as attractive to me without makeup or fancy dress, like how she looked first thing in the morning as she'd just risen from bed, compared to how she usually painted her face outside for the benefit of strangers. I discovered this during the first time she stayed over at my house, and I saw her morning face before she had a chance to prepare it for public viewing. The version of her face she made up for the world to see was fine, to be sure. There was nothing wrong with it. It was an amalgamation of traits she had been influenced to think were beautiful in her environment and that most people would respond positively to. But it was not a face that was an accurate representation of her. When I saw how she really looked, who she really was in her natural state without the glitz and glamor she hid behind, I knew it was a face I would want to wake up to every morning, a face I would want to see evolve and grow for decades. How could I have ever felt that way about her public, artificial face? Any other generically pretty girl could put the same effort into looking approximately the same and satisfying the same widespread social requirements for beauty.

My love seemed confused and even offended when I told her that, to me, she was already the most beautiful she could possibly be before altering her appearance. Any work she did would only detract from our exceptional physical chemistry. I was already 100% attracted to her. I saw then that, to her, beauty was value she thought she was supposed to work for—a gift she crafted for my and the world's benefit. Telling her that she was already the epitome of beauty to me without doing any of that work robbed her of what she saw as her feminine contribution. This poor, beautiful creature had been conditioned into believing that being beautiful meant giving up everything that made her look like herself. If only she could have seen that there was never a thing she needed to do to impress me or be the most beautiful woman in the world.

In the course of sharing a life with someone, you will see them in moments when they have not prepared their appearance: no makeup or fancy dress to craft the image designed to attract you. You will see them at their worst, just as they will see the same from you. If you are only attracted to them at a manufactured best, you're not really attracted to them at all. When you cannot help but still be drawn to them in physical form, even when it is not obvious that you should be, and even when no other men notice the beauty that you do, you will know you have found an incredible level of physical chemistry.

CHAPTER 4

The Sexual Burden

"When in love, the sight of the beloved has a completeness which no words and no embrace can match: a completeness which only the act of making love can temporarily accommodate."

— John Berger, *Ways of Seeing*
(Penguin Books, 1972)

Sex: this funny yet profoundly important little thing we do sometimes where we smoosh our genitals together because it feels good. How we engage in sex displays and embellishes our gender-specific qualities, both physically and emotionally, more than any other activity. The chemistry and synergy between men and women show up here more intimately than anywhere else. The emotions you feel when you're engaged in the sexual act help you know yourself better, and the act can be more therapeutic and stimulating for you and your partner than anything else you could experience. But you will never see everything sex is capable of becoming if you insist on treating it as mere genital stimulation.

Sex *is* genital stimulation, of course. There's a reason we have such sensitive and pleasurable parts on our bodies. Genitals evolved to be stimulated. But if sex were *merely* pleasurable genital stimulation, it would be little more than a glorified massage. And there'd be nothing wrong with that. A massage from someone you like, trust, and care about is wonderful. But if we just think of sex as solely a massage, we close off the possibility of it becoming more. We ignore that it can be a loving, bonding, spiritually uplifting experience—the peak of human experience, even. That's a pretty impressive outcome for such an animalistic aspect of our existence.

Dysfunctional sex is emblematic of the broader problems between men and women. If you can figure out how to have healthy, mature sex that is mutually rewarding, a lot of emotional and social problems will dissipate. It's like learning how to eat well. Your physical health is going to improve if you start to get better nutrition and less junk in your diet, no matter how else you live your life. If you could solve the sex problem and teach the average man and woman to have meaningful, deep, rewarding, healthy sex, a lot of the issues stemming from the dichotomy between masculinity and femininity would lessen.

Under healthy conditions of self-exploration and self-expression, every individual would be free to determine what role this drive will play in their lives. So why is it so common to discourage sexual impulse and activity much more than all other natural biological drives and functions?

We spend the early portion of our lives not experiencing any significant sexual drive. Teenagers entering puberty are usually the first to show strong sexual interest in others and feel the physiological effects. Maybe that's why we associate non-sexuality with innocence—because it is characteristic of childhood, which is not true of any other biological drive like hunger or sleep. Rather than seeing sexuality as a normal and healthy thing that just happens to take about 13 years to start to show up in most people, we might default to viewing the non-sexual starting conditions of childhood as the healthy norm. We might erroneously assume that adults should seek to maintain non-sexuality as a rule because it symbolizes a loss of those "pure" conditions we all started in. The fruit of the Tree of the Knowledge of Good and Evil mythos, as found in the biblical book of Genesis regarding Adam and Eve's expulsion from the Garden of Eden, captures this perspective well. For something more contemporary, refer to Brad and Janet's descent into sexual deviance in *The Rocky Horror Picture Show*. Life can never be the same once the apple has been eaten and sex is now an unignorable part of a maturing life. Once you are aware that you are a sexual being, you cannot return to being non-sexual. Pandora's box (pun proudly intended) cannot be sealed.

Touch-a touch-a touch-a touch me, indeed.

In the age of enlightenment and information, lesser-developed societies still do their best to restrict the flow of information about what sex is and how it works, even on an objective and scientific level. The thinking seems to go that the less people know about how their bodies work, the less capable they will be of using them in risky and impermissible ways. And the less awareness they have of other paradigms about healthy sexual expression, the less they will know to even question the narrow one they've been given. All this cultural superstition built up around sex—as a concept, as an act, as a sanctimonious set of values—leads to large populations fearing the lifelong consequences of rushing into a sensitive activity without fully understanding it. Some of this fear is justified. Reckless sex can change life for the worse. Then again, so can reckless anything, even driving to work. The best defense against inherent risks lies in greater education about how they work. If you don't want to die from obesity and heart disease, it will behoove you to learn which foods and lifestyle factors contribute most to those risks. If you wish to avoid getting pregnant, acquiring an STD, or getting emotionally addicted to sex, it would similarly behoove you to learn which negligent sexual behaviors lead to these outcomes.

Even in the West, parents revealing the nature of sex to innocent ears is often relegated to a singular taboo conversation where little significant wisdom or personal experience is communicated. We still call it "*the* talk" with the definite article, implying there's only one. You know. That thing that a man and woman do sometimes alone in their bedroom when they love each other very, very much. Not a fundamental process in the human body and psyche, one shared by the entire animal kingdom, the wondrous drive that makes the circle of life go 'round. I have never understood why sex had to be discussed any differently than any other fact of life, why it couldn't be explained as clearly and fairly as possible, as an open subject for discussion, in language that children or teenagers can understand as soon as they are interested in learning.

Maybe the magic of sex is how it takes something inherently gross and transmutes it into something enticing, something irresistibly appealing under just the right conditions with the right person. We normally don't go around sticking our fingers in other people's mouths or our genitals into someone else's for obvious reasons related to sanitation. And maybe sex *should* be gross most of the time. We shouldn't want to swap our bodily fluids with every remotely attractive person we encounter. Through some kind of biological wizardry, conditions can be just right such that we come into close contact with someone with whom the extreme grossness turns into equally extreme and mutual attraction. Suddenly, we *want* to be inside this person or have them inside us. We want to smell their sweat on us and taste their saliva. We want to be pumped full of or covered in the grossest products of their biology. And when it happens in just the right way with just the right person, it's the most magical experience in the world. Grossness transmutes into love, care, excitement, and affection.

In my exploration of the role this biological impulse plays in my life, I've made love to women I was deeply in love with and convinced I would spend the rest of my life with. I've also been in love with and physically attracted to someone I felt so disrespected by that I could never get comfortable enough to make love to. I've had intense fucking sessions with physically attractive strangers I hardly knew. Some of these were surprisingly rewarding because of the novel perspective they brought. It's nice to know what different types of women's bodies feel like pressed against mine. But many were also disappointing. I've had sex with women who displayed a stronger sex drive than me, only to find the experience of being with them mostly mechanical. Touch here. Rub there. Lick and suck every which way that you're supposed to. Now, harder and faster until we're done. Intimacy is overrated. Thanks for that. Same time next week? I've had sex with what I thought were timid and homely maidens who surprised me with how expressive and outgoing they became once they felt comfortable enough to activate all their emotions around me. In sex, they find the freedom to be whoever and do whatever they want. I've had sex with women more than 20 years my senior and more than 10 years my junior. From age gaps in both directions, I learned how you can sometimes see the youthful spirit in the older woman and the old soul in the younger one. I've had sex with friends who became much more to me than just friends but with whom I didn't exactly fall in love.

Sometimes this has worked out well for both of us, and sometimes it has ruined long-standing friendships. I've even fallen in love with my soulmate without ever seeing her naked or touching her in any manner more intimate than a prolonged embrace and kiss.

Despite my deep romantic leanings, I do not at all intend to denigrate casual sex in principle. Quite the opposite, in fact. "Casual sex" means sex that occurs without the expectation of a committed relationship. That's it. It doesn't mean it can't be intimate. It doesn't mean you can't respect and care for the person you do it with (indeed, you probably should). Ironically, casual sex doesn't have to be casual at all. But you also certainly don't need to be in love with this person for the sex to be a mutually rewarding and meaningful experience. You just need to be two people who both recognize that sex would be enjoyable but that entering a committed romantic relationship with each other would not. It's that simple. The set of all possible mutually rewarding sexual partners for you is certainly much larger than the set of all people who would make for good long-term monogamous partners.

As a romantically oriented man, I would certainly prefer to spend every day and share my bed every night with the woman I'm hopelessly in love with and committed to. But if I don't have that person in my life, who am I harming by having mutually rewarding sex with someone I'm not going to spend the rest of my life with? The biggest potential issue is that either partner might not be mature enough to communicate and handle the situation appropriately. As well, it's possible that the pursuit of casual sex (or the psychological effects of having it) could interfere with the pursuit of the higher priority of romantic monogamy. Then again, if employed correctly, it could enhance it. The romantic lessons that have come from so-called casual sex have been among my greatest in life. I've had plenty of casual sex, and I'm still the most romantic man I know. I'm more dedicated than ever to spending my life with one person I deeply love and can bond with on all conceivable levels. The greater the variety of sex I experience, the more it makes me appreciate that there is still a higher standard I aspire to, someone I will choose to be with for the rest of my life, physically and emotionally, because it will always be more rewarding than all the sexual novelty I could ever experience with other women.

I'm grateful for all my sexual experiences, even the bad ones. They have only prepared me to understand myself, the sexual act, and what my standards are. The quality of any given encounter comes from the matching or mismatching of expectations. The fact that two people are in a relationship and committed to each other doesn't automatically make sex rewarding, spiritual, transformational, transcendent, or anything like that. Your unique chemistry with your partner, combined with your willingness to trust and be vulnerable with each other, does that. The only conclusion I can draw from what I have witnessed in others and experienced within myself is that there is no singularly correct answer about the best way to express sexuality except that which most aligns with each person's values and personality. No universal cultural mandate about appropriate sexual expression will apply to everyone the same. It cannot remain relegated to a secret, shameful act that everyone participates in but few openly acknowledge, a taboo to be ignored but for a few fleeting moments under covers and in darkness. It's a fundamental part of how our bodies operate and how our psychology has evolved. It is a sensitive type of conversation between trusting partners. No conversation between any two participants will be exactly the same as a conversation between any two others. That's part of what makes the act so personal and special: You don't know exactly what you're getting into with each new partner, and finding out is half the fun.

THE CHAOS OF EARLY SEXUAL EXPLORATION

I, like all teenage boys, once suffered from a very crude interpretation of my sexual impulses toward women, but I was fortunate to be in conditions to overcome my sexual immaturity quickly. My first time having sex in high school went as well as I could have hoped for. I feel lucky in that regard. I hear a lot of horror stories from both men and women about how awkward and disappointing their first times were. I was spared that because I was in love with my first partner. Let's call her Juno. She was my first serious girlfriend (my proverbial "high school sweetheart"), and I was convinced I would marry her someday. She was a slim, plain, and sweet-looking brunette who became a stabilizing influence during my chaotic masculine development, my transition from boy to man. If she were an element, she'd be *earth*,[25] and I was the *air*[26] floating high over her, coming down to take root in her. She gave me my first true semblance of a place to belong in the world, so much so that I feared what I would become if I ever lost her and was left adrift again.

Our first time together was long-awaited by both of us and was a good experience because of the intensity of love and care between us, two idealistic youngins who had no reason to expect much due to our mutual inexperience. Juno told me that she enjoyed our first sex simply because it was us and it was real. It

---

25 *Earth is the element associated with stability, grounding, practicality, and endurance. It embodies the notion of foundation and provides a sense of security and rootedness.*

26 *Air is the element associated with intellect, thought, ideas, mental clarity, and communication. It prioritizes freedom, movement, and expansion of consciousness.*

wasn't a showcase to prove our skills at pleasing one another or a challenge for me to last as long as possible. It was just an intense and intimate bonding experience. What more could teenage me and her have asked for? Pop culture's idea of a horny young boy losing his virginity is quite different from what I was fortunate enough to experience. It's supposed to be awkward, rushed, brief, and uncomfortable for everyone involved (at least, that's what my TV tells me). Women are in pain during it and left feeling trashy, used, and unsatisfied after. What a tragic way to get introduced to sexuality and have your future expectations set.

I will be forever grateful that my first sex was with someone I loved so much and could indulge wholeheartedly into the act with. But many of my other formative experiences of intimacy did not happen under the conditions of love or even a committed relationship—yet each was uniquely meaningful and taught me important things about what was possible from sex.

Minerva, a tall, freckled blonde, was my oldest friend. If she were an element, she would be *water*[27]—calm, cooling, accepting, and soothing to me in all ways. There was always an attraction between us, of course. We both knew it but never talked openly about it. We were always partnered up with other people, so there was never really an opportunity for us to explore the possibility of being together in that way. Perhaps that limit to our interaction is what allowed us to develop something resembling a pure familial bond.

Then, the inevitable eventually happened (as inevitable things tend to do). As young adults, we were alone in her house one night, the same house I had seen her grow up in, and somewhat aided by alcohol, began to explore the one thing we had never

---

27 *Water is the element associated with fluidity, adaptability, support, and healing. It embodies sensitivity, empathy, and intuition.*

explored before. She kissed me. I kissed her. We locked eyes and both knew what we were doing with each other. There was no question about it. And as we tore at each other's clothes that night and explored each other's naked bodies for the first time, I mostly just thought how beautiful the moment was to me. The final piece of her was now available to me. I had seen every other side of this person, practically shared a life with her. I had been through such a great deal and bonded with her in every other way but sexually or romantically. Now, at last, I felt like I fully, truly knew her. I had the one piece I had been missing. And I loved her for it.

You can probably guess where this is going.

Nothing was the same the next morning. Minerva told me that what happened the night before had made her uncomfortable and that she would prefer we keep things the way they were before we acted on our long-latent sexual interest. I agreed despite deeply valuing what we experienced together. I obviously didn't want to do anything that would make my oldest friend in the world uncomfortable. In the weeks that followed, no matter how much she claimed the opposite, that she was not interested in any further sex or romance with me, my dear friend Minerva continued returning to me under similarly spontaneous conditions as our first night together, always ending up in my arms, kissing me, and removing my clothing. On our fifth recurring encounter, something finally snapped in her. She got off of me, hurriedly threw on her clothes in the middle of the act, leaving me naked and alone.

I never saw Minerva again after that. I only received one short phone call from her weeks later. Her tone was neutral. She wanted to check on me. That's all. I told her the truth: that I was upset and felt that I had been abandoned by her. It seemed she didn't know how to respond. But very deliberately, I made one thing clear in that final conversation: Whenever she would be ready to talk about what happened between us, I would always be there for her to do so. That's how important my friend of so many years was to me. My attempts to reach out to her after that were ignored. I felt a little part of me die with her. The most real family I had ever known was gone. A decade of friendship simply washed out of my life because someone I deeply loved was unwilling to have an uncomfortable conversation with me about the intimacy we shared.

What a way to end a friendship. At least we went out with a bang.

My theory is that Minerva's mental image of me broke because she no longer knew how to categorize our relationship. I don't think she was falling in love with me, exactly. I wasn't her type or her mine. I think she loved me in a way she did not have a blueprint for how to express. She relied too much on what the world around us told us were the correct ways for men and women to interact. Anything outside those boundaries was dangerous and unknown. So, what could have been an extremely rare and valuable expression of love existing across all categories between two people who understood and appreciated each other far better than almost anyone ever gets to became something unfathomable to her. Her mind simply couldn't process it.

I don't believe it was the sex itself that ruined our friendship. I know it is possible for two mature adults to remain friends once they have been physically intimate. It was Minerva's emotional immaturity and inability to process the intensity of what we shared that did us in. I know that had she been mentally prepared to communicate openly about what transpired between us, our friendship would certainly have been salvageable. Even if we never became intimate again or attempted to push our relationship to another level, we would have still held on to that infinitely valuable shared identification built over years of growing up together and bonding. Though I resented Minerva for years for what I saw as abandoning me, I eventually came to see that it was only because of how scared and fragile she was that she was capable of making that sacrifice at all. In the end, I pitied her for being such a bad friend to me.

As it was for Chandler and Monica, my sexual experience with Minerva was special because of how intimately I knew her and cared for her in all other areas of life before we ever indulged in lust. But there was another opportunity for early sexual exploration that affected me deeply for almost wholly lustful reasons. If being with Minerva was like cooling, flowing water, being with Venus, a short and fit redhead, was like a raging *fire*[28] quickly stoked between maturing bodies who had no idea how to handle the heat they were generating.

Before things ever turned sexual, there was always tension between me and Venus. Nothing was ever neutral in our frenemyship.[29] We bickered in conversation. Passion was always present in some form. That tension, built up in our daily social interactions, found a natural outlet through our private nighttime activities. We were quick to begin aggressively exploring and stimulating each other's bodies as we each learned about the other's teenage anatomy. Together, we made natural friction. I began to be turned on by almost everything about her physical presence, even though she probably didn't look particularly noteworthy to most men. What lingered most in my memory was

---

28 *Fire is the element associated with energy, passion, transformation, vitality, enthusiasm, and assertiveness. It's about wholeheartedly indulging our deepest desires without reservation.*

29 *"Frenemy" is a neologistic portmanteau of "friend" and "enemy."*

the way she smelled and the way our skin felt together. It was the first time in my young life that I experienced my entire body as a functioning sexual organ instead of just the concentration of nerves in my genitals. There's a lesson here about the power of pure physical chemistry and the all-consuming lust it can induce if wholly indulged without apology or reservation.

For years after we lost touch, I wondered if the early lustful experiences I shared with Venus were as meaningful to her as they were to me. Perhaps what I remembered about them had become embellished in my memory. Was I making it out to be more than it was? It's a question I likely would have had to live with for the rest of my life had Venus not reached out to me again one day. From her, I finally confirmed that our youthful sexual exploration had, indeed, stayed burned in her memory as it had in mine, despite each of us having had plenty of additional experience since then. There was just something magical about our particular physical pairing at that particular time in our lives when we were most sensitive to our developing libidos. Lightning in a bottle. How could either of us have known that the standard we set with each other back then would linger in our memories and shape our ongoing sexpectations? No one taught us about the emotional power of sex and how to manage its lasting imprint. I wonder if any of the adults around us even knew, if any of them were remotely self-expressed enough in this domain to be able to guide us if they had been willing to.

What made these youthful sexual experiences so meaningful was the purity of expression common among them. In each pairing with one of my goddesses, the two of us were doing exactly what we wanted to do to and with each other. I think that gets harder to experience as we get older and grow jaded by experience, even if we start to know our way around the opposite sex's physiology a little better. Back then, our actions were driven by primordial instinct instead of preconceptions about how we should be attracted to or treat each other. We just knew how to respond to every little sign and motion passed between us. I learned from a young age that the best sexual encounters can be merely a matter of listening and responding to what your partner is communicating to you and ensuring you are communicating clearly with them.

THE CRUDE AND UNWIELDY MASCULINE LIBIDO

For most men, the sexual impulse is nearly always there—a hairpin trigger easily set off at even slight provocation, eager to be satisfied by stimulation and orgasm. The frequency or intensity varies, of course. Some men feel that they need to jerk off multiple times a day. Others can probably go weeks without it and hardly notice. Even if we don't consciously pursue sexual activity, we still have penises connected to our nervous systems. We still get erections, sometimes seemingly at random. We still respond to visually arousing women. We still dream and fantasize. Denying the masculine sexual impulse is not easy—practically impossible. There's a reason certain types of monks have to forego all interaction with women if they want to keep their thoughts and focus pure. Even the Buddha concurred.

"Sex as a desire has no equal. Fortunately, there is no other like it. If there were, no one in the world would be able to cultivate the Way."

— The Buddha

Sexual stimulation brings a man into the present, into his body more than any other activity. Joy and beauty live only here, now. The right woman's mere presence already does a great deal to bring a man here with her in the now, where she naturally resides as experience embodied. Sex with her allows him to experience all of her on the deepest level while stimulating his most sensitive parts. That's the power women embracing their femininity hold over us, and we hope every day that they realize it and wield this power responsibly. There are no substitutes.

Even when I masturbate, I usually want the act to be over as quickly as possible. It's not something I need to savor. I just want the itch scratched so I can get back to doing more important things. But when I have sex with a woman, I want the experience of being with her to last as long as possible. I'm not doing it just for stimulation. I'm doing it to experience her—her body, her mind, her responses to how I touch her. It's a feedback loop. I receive pleasure by giving it, and I get even more by seeing how much my partner likes giving it to me, compounding the experience for both of us. Masturbation is overall a strangely casual and disgusting habit for men, not too far removed from picking one's nose. Most women can't imagine it happening so flippantly and frequently. It's a much bigger event for them if they even feel comfortable doing it at all. Even many highly sexual women I've known couldn't bring themselves into the right headspace to touch themselves the way they wanted a partner to touch them.

The internet has exacerbated the superficiality of the masculine libido by making it too convenient for us to see any type of woman naked. With just a few keystrokes and mouse clicks, any man can see a woman with virtually any combination of features he fancies naked. The wildest and most unattainable sexual fantasies of our crudest ancestors are now modern virtual realities. Now, there is only the final remaining link in the chain of truly immersive VR technology and generative AI to perfectly simulate the sexual act with the girls of our dreams. Star Trek holodeck orgies may already be the sexual norm by the time you read this. I can only wonder how the adoption of this technology will affect the world's gender-based sexual power dynamics, as men will no longer rely on real women to satisfy their overwhelming sexual curiosity.

Modern cavemen often fail to realize that most women have the capacity to experience sexual desire more deeply than men. It's less obvious because the feminine sex drive is not as broad and ubiquitous as the masculine variant. It's not always there, nagging at their consciousness like hunger or exhaustion. A woman typically needs to enter a certain headspace to feel it. She needs to feel safe with herself and her partner. Pornography designed for women usually mimics the conditions that make a woman feel safe and comfortable enough to indulge in sexual pleasure. Romantic movies and novels do the same. A penis is just a penis, and a man's body is just a body until the right psychological conditions are met. Then she cannot ignore it anymore and indulges.

Meanwhile, the common man can be overcome by the urge to fuck someone or touch himself to completion at random times. While he's eating or driving. While he's on a work call. When he spots a particularly attractive woman walking down the street, in a selfie online, or on a billboard on his way to school. The masculine libido has a crude and unwieldy mind of its own, not bound by courtesy and social norms. This is the reality that teenage boys all over the world start to experience when their sex drive kicks into gear during puberty and they become slaves to their surging hormones. A strange new force enters their lives that they will have to contend with for so long as their genitals remain operational.

If women naturally hold sex to a higher standard than men, perhaps it is men who should seek to live up to women in the bedroom instead of trying to drag them down to their level. The right man can even show a woman a standard she didn't even know she had. Perhaps she has only ever been disappointed with her direct sexual experiences with men but never understood why. No common man could demonstrate to her a truly rewarding sexual experience until the right one came along. Gentlemen, seek to be that uncommon man. You'll help move the human race along by setting a higher standard that other men must live up to.

The sexual experience is far more localized for men than women. Sexual stimulation is located predominantly in the penis. For some men, it may be the only place they feel it at all, as the rest of the body exists to operate as dense and dull machinery. So much of a prototypical man's capacity to feel is contained in his dick and, therefore, so much of his identity. An entire sector of his personality exists there. That's why a man wants a woman to just touch his goddamn penis so badly sometimes, like a drug addict seeking his next fix. Women can quickly infer this about a man when they see how drastically his personality changes once his penis is stimulated. It's one easy way for a physically weaker woman to dominate a man: by exploiting his most sensitive part. It's virtually impossible for most men to care about anything else during this time. A woman might as well be stimulating a man's whole body, including his heart, when she stimulates his dick.

It's why I've never liked wearing condoms. I understand what an important piece of preventative technology they are. But every time I wear one, my genital sensitivity drops dramatically, and it is significantly harder for me to be intimately invested in the sexual act. For peak physical intimacy, it's a good idea to reach a point where a couple is comfortable having unprotected sex, which means that the responsibility falls on men to be reliable enough not to prematurely ejaculate. It also means people need to be more selective about who they sleep with. Still, I understand completely when women insist on using condoms. I see how much trust they are putting in a man when they let him insert himself. The moment any woman indicates she would be more comfortable with a condom than without one, men should acquiesce.

A man's over-identification with his genitals can lead to understated insecurity about the size, shape, and general aesthetic quality of his penis. Because most men do not often view other men's genitals in person, most of their exposure to any but their own is likely to come from porn, which is hardly a fair sampling to compare to. The question worth asking is how much size matters to a particular woman for the intimacy and pleasure she will experience and what her ideal size might be. It's never a linear scale between size and sexual value. Fetishes aside, there's a limit to how much of a good thing you want. Women might have trouble understanding the psychological and egoic importance of a man's member because they lack a direct analog for it. Even the most attractive male model, in the best shape and with the most handsome face, will still be judged for his sexual prowess by the size and quality of his dick, which is not something he can directly influence and which is typically hidden from view until a woman has undressed him.

Because a prototypical woman's sexual responses are not nearly so localized to her genitals, she is more sensitive all over, which is something a dense and dull male body and the dense and dull mind accompanying it cannot empathize with at first.

A man can only begin to understand what the experience is like for her by observing the starkly different ways she responds to different types and locations of stimulation. A man must learn to focus on his whole body and hers during all phases of a sexual encounter. But if he is ignorant of the differences in male and female physiology and how they influence sexual psychology he will default to assuming that his sexual responses are mirrored in his female partner. If *he* enjoys repeated heavy stimulation in one localized spot between his legs, he figures *she* must like that, too. He touches her the way he wants her to touch him.

Counterintuitively, he must even let go of the obsession with trying to make a woman orgasm. She'll get there when she's ready in the way she's ready, so long as the whole-body communication is open and flowing between you. Orgasm is not always even an automatic goal. For men, orgasm is the period that comes (hehe) at the end of a sentence. It's the destination that the wild, twisting journey is leading up to. His challenge is to enjoy the journey as much as possible without being preoccupied with the end because the end is so easy to reach, even accidentally. Then, it's just a moment of bliss where nothing else could possibly matter. A few volcanic squirts of euphoria followed by embers and emptiness. It's not the point of the act; it just ends it. It's dessert after the meal. Sex should become more than a crank that produces ejaculation.

The feminine orgasm takes a woman deeper into what she is already doing. For many, there's not an abrupt distinction between cumming and not cumming. Some will not even be sure that they orgasmed because it could just be that they were deeply enraptured in non-orgasm and couldn't tell the difference. If a woman cums ten times effortlessly during a sexual encounter with you, it probably says a lot more about the woman and her body than it does about you and your sexual mastery. It's the same if you two can go for hours without her ever reaching climax but still wholly enjoying herself. This is why communication is so important. The way in which she reaches and experiences orgasm will be highly personal, so the burden is on her to communicate, subtly and overtly, how she wants her partner to touch and make love to her to bring her there. It is deeply unfair to a man to be expected to poke and prod his way around her sensitive bits until he stumbles upon the jackpot. A woman who whines about men's inability to make her cum has just revealed how bad she is at communicating her sexual needs to her partners.

Newsflash: Women Want Sex Too

All around the world, women can live their whole lives never seeing sex as anything more than an obligation to perform for their boyfriends and husbands. Their relationships are not based on love or sexual chemistry but on social convenience and cultural conformity. Under the most restrictive of conditions, they might never have experienced genuine sexual attraction toward a man, except perhaps as fanciful celebrity crushes. They have never indulged in the intimate closeness, the pull that overwhelms and brings bodies together that do not want to be apart. Unlike their male counterparts, women under these restrictive romantic conditions have barely even explored their capacity to experience lust toward the men they find physically attractive. One has to imagine how desolate the dating scene must be for entire generations of women to grow up not knowing it's possible or permissible for them to have and exert physical preferences about the men they take to bed, something they often see as crude, improper, and reserved solely for the bestial masculine psyche.

Women, like men, *are* sexual creatures, though typically not in quite the same way. That's one of the most important things that men who routinely fail at receiving or depend on manipulation to receive sex from them overlook. They'd have a lot more success if they could just approach women as equals with shared interests and goals, one of which might include a mutually rewarding sexual experience. Many women don't even understand this about themselves due to the sexually restrictive conditions they are reared in. They've scarcely had the opportunity to explore the role of sex in their lives. So, they just learn to function as best as possible without it.

One incredulous woman from a sexually repressed culture, after learning that I'd had many casual sexual partners, asked how I'd managed to *trick* them all into sleeping with me. My first instinct was to feel a bit offended at the idea that the only way women would ever agree to sleep with me was that they were tricked into it. However, I realized that her assumption had more to do with her stunted paradigm of female sexuality than it did with her perception of me. She had been raised to believe that women should naturally only want to have sex with the man they marry and only after they are married. Any woman who engages in premarital or casual sex couldn't possibly be doing it out of a rational decision to pursue her own pleasure in the way a man does.

In my experience, most women, especially those from sexually repressive cultures, are just looking for someone they can feel comfortable enough around to have a good sexual experience with, which can be frustratingly rare depending on the general quality of men around them. Trust and a base level of physical attraction are enough for many of them. It doesn't have to be love. It doesn't have to be wild, passionate, or mind-blowing attraction. It can just be someone you feel good about getting to know in this way and sharing yourself with. Far more women, in fact, have used *me* for sex than the other way around.

Trust seems to be the most difficult criterion for most men to meet because they have been trained to see the act of bedding women as manipulative. Many of them *do* have to trick women into sleeping with them because they don't believe they would otherwise have any reason to. Ironically, the very woman who acted so incredulous that so many women would be the one to initiate a sexual encounter would go on to use me as an opportunity for sexual exploration once she felt comfortable expressing herself as a sexual being around me, spontaneously deciding one morning that she wanted to experience a real-life, honest-to-goodness, human dick before quickly cutting off contact with me. It's hard not to feel used in such a situation, especially when you consider what the social response to a man treating a woman in an equivalent manner would (and rightfully should) be.

Women may be more reluctant to admit their casual interest in sex because they are subject to greater social scrutiny for it. This is primarily a projection from men who don't want to think of the women they want to marry as crude, sexual beasts like they are. Most men are actually quite ashamed of their own animalistic sexuality. They can't just accept that they have bodies with primal needs that coexist with everything sophisticated and human about them. This creates an absurd social situation wherein men are praised for participating in sexual acts, and women are shamed for the same. So when a sexually interested woman under such conditions meets a man she feels will accept her interest without shaming her, she feels good about exploring this side of herself with him. It's ironic that the stereotypical assumption is that men are most often looking to use women for short-term, consequence-free sexual thrills. Women want sexual experience just as much as men, though they tend to have a much harder time finding it due to the cultural stigmas that apply to them and the lack of quality male sexual partners to choose from.

Appropriately, some of my least rewarding sexual experiences have been with women who treated the sexual act like common men do. These disappointments have allowed me to empathize with women who regularly endure similar un-intimate encounters with the men they take to bed, seemingly without a better option in sight. I am attracted to women who show me their softness and sweetness. I naturally melt into them physically if conditions are right. Sexual intercourse is just a natural extension of that. So, I'm quite surprised and disappointed if such women suddenly take on a more stereotypically masculine, forceful, and rushed approach to intimacy. These are women who just want a dick in them for a little while, and, apparently, using a broom handle or some other phallic implement to serve the purpose would be too crude. They would rather objectify me—to literally use me as an object for their own pleasure. The ideal pairing would be between women who just want a dick in them and men who just want to put their dick somewhere for a few minutes. Both can walk away satisfied with their pitiful encounter. Disaster strikes, however, when one side of the pairing has higher, more intimate ambitions and is left feeling trashy and used once the act is over.

Now, obviously, every woman is entitled to her own preferences for sexual activity. The fact that some women's idea of a good time in bed is different than my own is immaterial. What's noteworthy here is the immediate expectation that sex could *only* happen in the narrow way they preferred it. It implies to me that it's the only way they've ever experienced it—the only way they know that it can go. This is what they think sex is. Therefore, *I'm* doing something wrong if I don't conform to it. There's no communication or the reaching of shared expectations together. There is no push and pull, action and reaction. Therefore, there is no intimacy. It's a fossilized conception of sex that overwrites any novel experience, even as it's happening right in front of and inside them in real-time.

I've seen this happen even with women who were soft, feminine, and intimate everywhere outside of the bedroom. Flirtatious banter in the kitchen. Moments holding each other on the couch. Falling asleep on each other's shoulders while an uninteresting movie plays in the background. But then, almost as soon as the possibility of genital stimulation or penetration becomes involved, the whole emotional tone of the encounter changes. "Sex" takes on its own compartmentalized category, completely unrelated to the subtle intimacy we shared until then. They do not see intercourse as an extension of everything that came before and our unique relation to one another. They have been conditioned to force it to happen in a certain shallow way.

The best explanation I can come up with for this common dichotomy is that emotional intimacy combined with sexual stimulation is too much sensitivity to bear. If they are not fully free to feel and express themselves, this peak of vulnerability will overwhelm them. A mature man can introduce a woman in such a limited state of mind to a deeper level of sex and intimacy, but only if it is clear she is ready for it and willing to go deeper than what she has known before. And if she trusts him to be the one to show her the way.

How Men Can Acquire Sex Without Manipulation[30]

For men, sex is often a form of conquest over women, as though they have accomplished something by tricking a reluctant or

---

30 *Or: How to Get Laid More, Ethically*

prude woman into sleeping with them. And typically, once they have satisfied that sexual curiosity, their interest falls. They set women's expectations for something more, like love or a relationship, because they believe it is the only way to get them to agree to have sex. Disappointment and even heartbreak follow, and many vulnerable young women have been scarred for life by horny young men who did not realize the destruction they were causing by being dishonest to satisfy their lust. As far as I'm concerned, this is not much better than physically forcing sex on women. It's rape by psychological means—sex consented to under false pretenses.

Ask the women you know if they have to worry about men suddenly ceasing to talk to them after sleeping with them for the first time. It seems like such a strange, widespread behavior. You want to sleep with a girl you find attractive. You may put months or years of effort into convincing her to do it with you. Then, instead of continuing to sleep with her and reaping the rewards of all your effort, you immediately disconnect and start the cycle over again with a new target. Wouldn't it be a much wiser investment of time to continue having sex with a woman at least a few times before running off to the next one? Ask these poor women what these one-off sexual experiences were like. The answer will always be that they felt their bodies were used by these men for their own pleasure. The encounters were quick, shallow, and degrading.

Because sex is so vital to the healthy functioning of masculine psyche, it is an important lifestyle skill for men to be able to acquire it in a mature and mutually beneficial way with women. It is also a necessary component of the masculine maturation process to stop seeing sex as something women have total exclusive power over and dole out at their narrow discretion to the relatively few men who do enough to earn their shallow attention. Sex is all around you, like air or conversation—if you know how to find it.

There isn't a universal approach to acquiring sex from women that works for every man with every woman in every situation. Though many have tried, no one could write a worthwhile manual that simply tells you, "Touch a woman here, here, and here to give her the best sex of her life. Compliment her in exactly this way. Wear exactly this and do these four things to impress and seduce her." There are only principles that generally describe how things work. You just start noticing patterns if you've done this enough times with enough women under a broad enough variety of conditions. Indeed, part of the appeal of a deeper intimate relationship with one woman is learning all the personal things about her that don't conform to broader generalization. Your interaction with her evolves to be more bespoke the longer you spend with her and the deeper you connect.

Describing how to make love is like describing how to have a good conversation with someone. That will depend on the particular people involved in it. Frankly, some pairings of people could probably never result in a good conversation, and they shouldn't try to force it to happen. Meanwhile, some pairings will align such that they stay up all night effortlessly talking without being instructed how to. How they talk will be unique to them, and it might not have much in common with how most other people talk. Sex is just whole-body communication. When communication is good, sex is good. In most cases, it's very easy to predict what sex with someone is going to be like because it's just like having a conversation with them. However you talk to each other is what it's going to be like in bed between you. If you want to know what sex with me is like, you should already be getting a pretty good idea of it just by reading this book.

A basic philosophy of sex is to do a simple thing very well. In most cases, elaborate flourishings infused upon the act are not required for a satisfying experience. Most women don't care about the variety of techniques you are programmed in or whether you can fulfill some secret fetish. They want your attention, from your whole body to theirs. They want you to take the appropriate time and carefully make every motion, however minor. It's the sexual equivalent of a basic home-cooked meal made with love. You don't need expert chopping and dicing techniques and spice combinations to pull this off. You just need to be confident in who you are, the tools and ingredients you are working with, and the outcome you are working toward with your partner. Whole body care and attention go much further than any other quality in the bedroom.

You don't even have to be particularly attractive as a man to get laid. We are fortunate in that regard. At a minimum, all you have to do is not be gross. Certainly, it's an advantage to be handsome, but unless you just happen to be born that way, maintaining handsomeness requires a hell of a lot of vanity and attention to every aspect of dress and grooming. And any woman who seeks out only the hottest guys that all other women generally want to have sex with is probably not a woman of high character. Instead, just focus on not being gross. That's enough for most women to be sexually enticed if all other conditions can be met. And gross is pretty easy to identify.

It's a truth universally acknowledged that women tend to be attracted to men taller than them. The tallest women, therefore, have the smallest available dating pool of men even taller than them. This is an inescapable consequence of height distribution. A similar dynamic happens with age. One less-acknowledged truth is that women are also almost always attracted to men a bit *smarter* than they are. Imagine the limited options for extremely smart women. No matter what other attractive qualities a man might have, women don't want to feel like they've been paired with an idiot. They don't want to have to talk down to the man they look up to. A dumb man or one of even middling intelligence seems like a child to a brilliant woman. Many have even had to downplay their intelligence to appeal to men less bright than them. A man who is as smart as or smarter than a smart woman might be among the first in her life to encourage her to display her full intellect. He does not feel threatened by it. It's part of what he values in her. Finally, she feels like she can be herself and talk on the same level to someone she wants to get intimate with. Finally, she feels like she might gain something by listening to him. A related attraction dynamic exists for men she finds interesting, which, as noted, is closely related to how she feels about men she finds intelligent.

The job of a good man, if he wants his unignorable sexual burden met in a fair, honest, and ethical way, is to activate a woman emotionally before he activates her physically. Because he is almost always at least semi-active in the sexual domain, almost always ready to act on the opportunity for sex, he forgets that few women share this tendency. That's why foreplay is important. If she doesn't think she's in the mood but he starts kissing her neck just right and saying just the right things to her, she might suddenly become even more sexually activated than him. It's like an act of worship of her body. It's his way of showing that her body is the most wonderful thing he's ever seen. Experiencing it is a joy for him, his heaven or nirvana. *That's* what puts her in the mood: his initial interest passed into her.

Turning a man on rarely requires more than touching his penis, if even that. Male genitalia is external. It is clearly visible, easy to handle, and protrudes away from the body. Female genitalia disappears inside. A man is freer to view sex as something he does with an appendage he owns, a tool, a piece disconnected from the whole. A woman has no such luxury. Sex occurs *inside* her. She cannot avoid being physically vulnerable, no matter how dominant her personality. New sexual partners might even avoid vaginal stimulation and penetration for the longest time because they know how vulnerable such pleasure and the act required to create it would make them. The common man never considers these uncomfortable possibilities from a woman's perspective. He is too concerned with his own imperative, which is to thrust his way physically into something soft and warm that embraces him and feels good all around his most sensitive part.

There is also generally far greater variability to consider in what women will enjoy or *not* enjoy during a sexual encounter than men. Half the process is just figuring out the ideal way to touch and interact with her that she will respond to best. No matter how skilled, experienced, and confident he is, a man cannot rush in blind and assume he knows a new woman's body well. Exploration is essential. A man must observe what goes on in the woman as he works his way around her whole body. He may even accidentally discover several new, unexpectedly powerful ways of stimulating her. Perhaps she herself did not even know she would enjoy being touched that way until now, under just the right conditions, with a partner she feels comfortable and has the right chemistry with.

The consistent theme of ethical seduction is trust and comfort. That is the only non-manipulative way to turn a woman's body from an insensitive, non-sexual organism to a sensitive and sexual one. Otherwise, she stays closed off to you or starts to think of the sexual experience like a man. It ruins all the magic of the dichotomy between masculine and feminine coming together. A special moment occurs when a woman decides she trusts you enough to have sex with you for the first time. It's when she stops subtly ignoring your advances and starts overtly responding to them with her own. The process begins with you showing your intentions by the way you talk to and touch her in the places she allows you to. But still, she is depending on you to stop yourself from going where she is not ready based on how she responds to your initiation. Restraint is a powerful thing in a man because it means the woman gets to be the one to indulge. It shows her he can be trusted to stop or back off if she changes her mind about what is happening for any reason. Remember: She is necessarily vulnerable during the sexual act. His imperative is full steam ahead, but hers is cautious indulgence. She needs to know that he can be on the same page as her before she gives in to what he is doing to her. Sex can be so much more rewarding for a man when he lets her come to him this way, when he opens the door but lets her be the one to walk through it. He knows then that she definitely chose it. She wanted to push things there. She is not just responding politely to what he wants from her because she feels obligated to or wants to make him happy. She is pursuing her own happiness by engaging with him. And when two people can confidently do that together, rewarding sex and intimacy finally start to happen.

Trust is such a foreign concept to men in flirting and seduction because they are so often based on *misdirection*. A man says something ambiguous enough to be interpreted as benign, but that also hints at intimate and risky intentions. A woman obscures her level of interest in response to it. Both parties cautiously dance around each other as they inch closer to the shared truth of their desire. No one wants to risk just displaying what they mean upfront lest they be denied or judged. Men can stand out by being the self-confident exception to this rule. Knowing who you are and what you want means never having to feel ashamed if your intentions go unreciprocated or might be disapproved of by the surrounding culture. Transparency goes a long way toward building trust with women accustomed to having to see through the bullshit ordinary men spew at them. It's refreshing to interact with someone who simply says what he means and puts his intentions across as clearly as possible.

Feminine comfort comes from knowing what to expect. Knowing what to expect makes her less hesitant to express herself in a sexually dynamic way. Sex itself is a dynamic and sensitive form of self-expression. You make women comfortable by repeatedly demonstrating your character in ways they care about beyond superficial displays of courtesy. There's nothing inherently wrong with holding doors open for women or offering to carry heavy bags for them—so long as you're doing it as a genuine expression of the desire to help. But for many men, these courtesies are part of the flirtation and seduction racket. They are done primarily to influence women into having a higher opinion of the men who perform them, which might just ever so slightly increase the chances that those women might one day agree to go out or sleep with them. Your character shows through in better ways if you let it. Listen when women talk. Be consistent with what you claim to care about. Basically, let women feel like they know what to expect when dealing with you. Never give them a reason to think there might be some form of danger waiting beneath the surface of you if they make the mistake of getting too comfortable and letting their guard down.

A benefit of women naturally feeling more comfortable around you is the willingness to share increasingly sensitive details on intimate subjects. Sex is a domain where virtually every woman will have at least some fears, anxieties, traumas, or bad experiences that they generally can't express because the world would judge or attack them for doing so. If a woman is comfortable enough to talk to you about what she liked or didn't like in the past, what she hopes for or fears in the future, or her general approach to sexuality, it opens the door for you to be someone she feels comfortable exploring sexuality with. She won't be doing this because you have the biggest muscles or the most symmetrical face. She'll be doing it because you will have started to demonstrate to her that you are someone she has genuine compatibility with and who will prioritize her comfort during a sensitive activity. Listening earnestly to a woman's sexual thoughts and experiences also gives you vital information about what to do or (more likely) not to do as you grow closer to her. Perhaps she will tell how much she has always felt used by men for her body in relationships and during sex. Or she might reveal how men in the past manipulated her into doing things she wasn't comfortable doing by acting like she was obligated to. Hearing enough of these stories, you realize how easy it is to be better than the general competition of undeveloped men. You start to have much more sympathy for what modern women endure in their relationships with men.

A woman needs to feel safe with a man, and one of the best ways for her to do that is to know that other women already do. Social proof is a powerful sales tool. It's why you see men at the top of the sexual hierarchy frequently flaunting the quantity and quality of women they have been able to convince to spend time around them. If you talk about your past sexual partners in a way that suggests you manipulated women into sleeping with you or sought domination and control over them, it will turn good women off. But if you talk about them in a way that suggests women naturally feel safe expressing themselves around you, that you were a positive force in these women's lives, it will do the opposite. When mature men can learn that sexual attention from women does *not* have to be a scarce resource, the sexual power women laud over them will lessen. Masculine sexual mastery extends far beyond being "good in bed" and into all aspects of social interaction with women, everything from the first moment of attraction until well beyond the deal has been sealed and all the bases covered. You carry that maturity with you in all non-sexual settings, too.

BRIDGING THE AGE, MATURITY, OR EXPERIENCE GAP

Society has frequently applied a reductionist view to what it means to be an adult and capable of taking responsibility for mature decisions and their consequences. The story goes that the day a child reaches the age of consent,[31] they instantly become capable of mature decisions regarding sex. It's a binary absolute. Whatever happens between two "consenting adults" past this point is fair game, so the lore goes. Midnight on your 18th birthday is supposed to be logistically the same as any other age regarding sexual ethics. I have long been bewildered by the juxtaposition of ideas that women should be regarded as innocent and asexual children until their 18th birthdays and then prized and fetishized as soon as they are "barely legal," now culturally condoned to be treated as objects for men's sexual gratification. Sexualizing

---

31 *The legal age of consent is presently 18 in the USA, 14 to 18 in most of Europe, and as young as 11 or 12 in other parts of the world. These significant differences between when physical intimacy is considered a responsible expression of maturing sexuality or statutory rape should tell us something about how an absolute chronological standard for adulthood and responsibility fails to capture the nuances of individuals exploring sex at various stages of mental and physical development.*

someone 6,573 days old is one of the worst crimes a man can commit but deserves fist bumps and high-fives all around just 24 hours later. In reality, there can be teenagers with the maturity of someone much older, and there can be old farts who still act like children and should probably be regarded as such with sensitive matters like sex.

It's no great mystery why young women tend to be attracted to older men and young men tend to have the hardest time getting laid. Young men are out of their element when it comes to intimate interaction. The best an inexperienced young man can be is sincere in his intention and willing to undertake the sexual developmental journey. An older man is expected to have learned from the experiences of his youth about who he is, how sex works, and how to treat women. On the flip side, it seems a cruel trick of nature that men of all ages tend to be most physically attracted to women still largely in a state of psychological infancy. They are young adults but still little girls at heart, just barely figuring out who they are, how to live in the world, and how to treat other people responsibly—yet at the peak of their biological fertility and signaling as such in countless ways subtle and overt.

With an age gap, there will usually be an imbalance. The younger party will be at a psychological disadvantage due to their lesser experience and self-knowledge. An older man can too easily manipulate a younger woman because he likely knows how she works better than she does. A 35-year-old guy has learned things about an 18-year-old girl's psychology and biology, her mind and body, that she has not yet. He can exploit her needs and weaknesses. She has to be able to trust his intentions completely.

There's an enormous amount of responsibility that comes with being one of a young woman's first sexual experiences, especially the very first. You are showing her what it is possible for sex and intimacy to be and setting a standard that she may carry for a long time. She will probably never forget the first time a man she trusts touches her in an intimate way or the first time she explores his body in kind. An older, more mature, and more experienced man has to manage the expectations of his naïve and innocent partner to minimize the chance of emotional fallout in the aftermath if he is to risk taking on this responsibility. He must do everything in his power to make sure they are good memories and that she carries healthy sexual associations forward. She can gain a lot from his experience, but only if he is ready to offer it for her benefit.

There is a world of a difference between consent given based on superficial understanding and truly *informed* decision making. No matter how much curiosity about sex she shows, does the younger party have the capacity to fully understand what she is consenting to? Sex is an emotionally and physically sensitive act. That's why the potential for damage is so high. Intellect is not enough. With little experience in sex and romance, she will likely be overwhelmed by its consequences.

A sexually inexperienced woman likely has had many conflicting beliefs about sex instilled in her. Sometimes, she is desperate to break away from these limitations everyone around her applies to a domain they know little about. Or she may be curious enough to explore the possibilities but will quickly get in over her head when she is overwhelmed by arousal and stimulation. Her culture goes to war with what her body experiences, which can induce a trauma response, either during the act or long after. She may judge herself for the *sin* she has committed by indulging in natural drives. The older male suitor is the easy scapegoat during such an internal collapse, for surely it is he who has corrupted such an innocent angel who would never have experienced sexual temptation had he not manipulated her into it.

It doesn't make a lot of sense to try to have an equal relationship with someone half your age because you're simply not going to be equals. With great care, the mixed-age, -experience, or -maturity relationship can take on the form of a sexual mentorship. A mentorship lays the path for the younger party to become more mature while acknowledging the difference in the maturity between the two. Designating the relationship this way acknowledges the imbalance between the two instead of ignoring it and expecting things to work out fine anyway. If a man calls a woman half his age his girlfriend or partner, there is an expectation of equal power and responsibility. The young woman cannot easily live up to the standards of someone with twice as much life experience, and the old man cannot diminish himself down to the level of a youth. The task is to find the overlap that exists between them in their authentic states for them to both benefit from the encounter without being in denial about where they each are. This is in contrast to teen girls who date established men because it provides them a facsimile of maturity by association, or creepy old men who chase after college students because it makes them feel chipper again. The difference is self-honesty. A mentor is not manipulative because he explains what he knows to the furthest extent that his mentee will be able to understand it. He must have the temperament to approach his relationship with her cautiously for the purpose of preparing her to become more mature. He has to tell her why he's doing what he's doing and how it's going to affect her. It's only manipulative if he deceives her in some way, whether that's in the form of deliberately lying to her, not informing her of something she *should* know, or simply not correcting an erroneous premise she holds.

Less common, though potentially just as valuable, is the pairing of younger men with older, more experienced women (colloquially known as "cougars"). This pairing happens less often because both members are less likely to be attracted to each other. Younger men want younger women physically, and older women want older men psychologically. Typically, for this chemistry to work, it takes an unusually mature younger man and an unusually youthful older woman. The young man who doesn't act so much like a young man goes well with the old woman who doesn't look so much like an old woman. It's impressive when an older woman is still physically attractive because it's attractiveness as a consequence of the type of woman she's chosen to become, not the easy, default state of her bodily existence. I see plenty of attractive young women every time I leave my house and remember few of them. I remember the women ten or more years older than me who I can't manage to take my eyes off of.

Throughout my twenties, a great portion of the romantic interest I received came from somewhat older women who were drawn to my developed outlook, despite me looking quite young. I rarely dated someone my own age during those years. One used to tell me, "I would have loved to have met a guy as mature as you when I was your age." I responded, "I'm pretty sure you would have ignored me when you were my age, just like most of the women my age do." Then, sometime in my late twenties, the balance shifted. I got approached more by women five to ten years younger than me, the same type of young women who mostly ignored me when I was their age. From this, I learned that a more experienced woman can help an inexperienced man gain control over his body and see sex and intimacy from a broader perspective beyond the cute, hyperactive attraction of his nubile feminine peers. Young men fortunate enough to be involved with more mature women may be relieved to see that the volatility characteristic of feminine youth does not have to stick with a woman all her life. He learns what to look forward to if he sticks with one woman for a long time and they mature together.

There are benefits too for older men and women exploring sexuality with younger, inexperienced partners beyond the obvious of getting to take someone hot and fresh to bed. They get to re-experience the novelty of sexuality through the eyes of someone who hasn't experienced everything they already have many times over. They are reminded of how sensitive they were way back when all this was new and overwhelming. That's one of the benefits of all mixed-age interactions, romantic or otherwise. Each side sees the world just a bit through the other's perspective.

As with all intimate relationships, but especially so when there is an imbalance of power, expectations must be clearly set and communicated to avoid eventual collapse. I've entered into intimate encounters with younger women who believed they could approach our interactions like mature adults. The longer the interaction goes on, the more likely they are to eventually regress to a childlike psychological state and risk everything blowing up if they are not truly ready. The more experienced party must anticipate potential issues before they arise. They must communicate them to the less-experienced one and warn them of the dangers of going further down a path they cannot foresee the results of. They must also know when to back off or push things ever so slightly further once there is enough evidence to move forward. So long as the more vulnerable of the two is clearly learning and growing into a more confidently self-expressed version of themselves, the mutually beneficial encounter can go on.

It is one of the most heartbreaking experiences I know to see someone you care about, someone you are deeply invested in the growth and maturation of, regress into a volatile and infantile state after helping them come a long way toward being the person they are capable of being—to see an almost-woman regress into a tantrumming little girl because she was not ready for the emotional responsibility she took on by beginning to explore her sexuality. It feels like watching her die, or at least become the worst version of herself. It is a reminder that permanent growth is earned through repeated willful indulgence into experiences that challenge us to know ourselves more and become more in the process. It cannot be a product of one-time occurrences and exceptions to the rule of permissible behavior, such as the absurd global cultural idea that a girl becomes a woman and a boy becomes a man the first time they participate in genital smooshing, whether under the sanctioned conditions of a holy union under the eyes of God and society or in the unholy alleys of red light districts and society's sexual shadow.

CHAPTER 5

Love and the End of Sexual Curiosity

> *"There will always be a person who looks like a poem Earth wrote to keep you alive."*
>
> — Juansen Dizon

Every love has been different. It's impossible to directly compare them, to hold one as the standard all others must be measured against. If there is a unilateral standard to be applied, it is how comfortable I was with her... how understood and appreciated I felt... how much it finally seemed like I could be at peace in the world, resting and just letting myself be happy in her presence and her warmth. I can just be... happy... with her. My God—what a luxury. More than any other indicator, there has just been the peace being bonded to the right woman brings me. It is unmistakable; it is the state in which I stop searching for anything greater than what is happening.

Most wants are not sustainable in the long run. But that's not true if something is the best possible thing you could want, the thing that's most in line with your nature and your values. Novel curiosity rules the inexperienced mind. When a man fixates on a woman's physical characteristics, it's usually because she has something new and interesting about her that captivates him. He wants to see her body. He wants to experience it, if at all possible. But once he has satisfied that curiosity, his interest diminishes because she is no longer a mystery to solve or a novel physical experience. He knows where that road leads now, so he dedicates his attention to the next one.

When men have something like a midlife crisis and cheat on their wives with someone younger and hotter, it's often simply because they did not give themselves the freedom to become totally sexually fulfilled before dedicating themselves to one woman. They have not satisfied their sexual curiosity. It haunts them. When men cheat, it can be as simple and crude as the opportunity for a lustful experience in a moment of weakness. It does not necessarily imply that they are unsatisfied with their relationship. Novel curiosity runs its course until you act on it enough, and then it's gone. Novel curiosity can also be unrelenting until it is resolved. It nags at you if you try to ignore it, never truly leaving you. The only way out is through. You don't want to spend the rest of your life wondering what a certain experience would have been like if you had permitted yourself to explore it.

Being romantic does not disqualify a man from being promiscuous. Various intimate experiences have informed what kind of choices I make today about the person I want to spend my life with. I know with a level of confidence greater than most who I am and what makes for a good partnership for me. I could not have that if I had just married the first pretty girl I ever bonded with. The more perspective one has, the more meaningful each choice becomes and the more wisdom and responsibility are required. In other words: With experience comes higher standards. When you know what all kinds of women look like naked, how it feels to touch their bodies and be inside them, and how you intimately interact with them, you will know your truest preferences. You will know what you are looking for, what is sustainable for your interest and peace. You will seek that out as a priority over all passing curiosities.

I don't know that I ever would have been able to overcome the burden of my sexual curiosity if I had not had the opportunity to fully explore it with women of all shapes, sizes, colors, textures, and temperaments. As such, I hope every horny young man gets the opportunity to fuck women with bikini model bodies so that they get the nagging urge out of their system and realize there is more that they are looking for. I hope each young man stops simping[32] for women who merely look good naked because he has learned how limited that appeal is. When sex and feminine beauty cease to be magical, rare, and elusive things held over him like trophies, he will be free to focus on more important matters.

Romantic Indulgence and Discretion

I grew up in Southern California, which is probably one of the most sexually liberal places in the world. I used to associate with people who were convinced that everyone was secretly bisexual and polyamorous (meaning they wanted to have sex with both sexes and maintain active sexual relationships with many partners concurrently). Therefore, the only thing stopping everyone from having sex with everyone else is that they are too repressed to admit they want to. They, quite ironically, pride themselves on being open-minded but can't conceive of the possibility that the way

---

32 *"Simping" is a term that originated in internet slang and meme culture, referring to the act of overly idolizing or admiring someone to the point of self-denigration. In this case, it applies specifically to hopeless men who adore and compliment attractive women they have no hope of ever winning sexual reciprocity from. It's a common feature in parasocial and one-sided relationships.*

they express their own sexuality is not appropriate or authentic for everyone else. As such, the concept of voluntary monogamy, of truly wanting to dedicate yourself wholly and exclusively to just one person for the rest of your life, is an impossible idea in their paradigm. All couples cheat (or want to), so they seem to think. They are just bold enough to admit it to their partners.

When I was casually invited as a young man to a "cuddle party" by San Diego's most prominent polyamorous group, I had to ask the woman extending the invitation for clarification. I had never heard of such an unusual event. "A cuddle party... is that like a bunch of people hanging out on couches in pajamas or something?" She responded with a bit of winking nonchalance. "Yeah, something like that. You'll see when you get there."

It was *not* something like that. It was something quite different than that, in fact.

I arrived at the cuddle party to find a single large room with its floor covered in pillows, cushions, and mattresses. A group of about 30, mostly middle-aged men and women, filled the floor of the room in various states of partial undress. Being the youngest there made me the target of unwanted amorous attention from older men and women. I was the fresh meat of the group, which might have been the manipulative reason the woman who invited me failed to elaborate on exactly what the experience would entail. What I witnessed that night could best be described as a softcore orgy, with the only explicit rules being that full nudity, penetration, and fluid emission of any kind were not allowed at this particular event. You'll be pleased to know they had a separate, more hardcore type of "party" with fewer restrictions for those who were so inclined.

It's not my place to judge the private sexual habits of strangers, no matter how strange they might seem to me. But the fact that these people openly invited me and failed to give me fair warning about what I would endure there gives me some free license to share and criticize. It's my belief that this polyamorous community hoped the cuddle party experience would "awaken" some kind of rampant sexual desire in me that I was unaware of, just as it seems to have once been awakened in all of them. Even then, in my early twenties, I had already been free to examine and explore my sexuality. I knew who I was, what I was attracted to, what I lusted after, and what I wanted out of a sexual experience or romantic partner. I applied sexual discrimination in a way uniquely suited to my identity. It seemed to rile them that they couldn't influence me into giving that discretion up and joining them in their ambiguous omnisexuality: fucking all things at all times just because they could. This is the inverse problem of the global norm to repress sex under almost all conditions. Some vocal minority believes that any romantic discretion is a betrayal of one's nature. I've been molested by both men and women who thought this way, my molesters naively assuming that I'd welcome and encourage their sexual advances because I was a virile young man who, in their eyes, should have been interested in all sex all the time. It's a strange countercultural response, as though they seek only to embody the opposite of what repressive cultural authorities want for them.

Many such people have even shown skepticism when I claim that, as a heterosexual male, I have never felt the slightest sexual inclination toward another man. It doesn't matter how emotionally close I am with him or what he looks like. This is in stark contrast to the arousal process that activates in my body and mind when I see a woman of even slight appeal to me. I've always told myself that if I ever felt any kind of positive sexual response toward another man, I'd be honest and open-minded enough to explore it.

Thirty-five years and counting—it hasn't happened yet, and not for lack of opportunity. Especially when I was younger and had a bit more boyish charm, I was approached by many interested gay men, most of whom were respectful about the whole thing, but a few of whom took things in a very forward, very gross direction from the start. I started to imagine that this must be what heterosexual women have to deal with all the time from men they are not remotely interested in. That's a pretty good benchmark for how straight men can think about their interaction with women: If you wouldn't be comfortable with a gay man saying or doing something to you, you can probably assume some random woman would feel the same about you acting the same toward them. There's no reason to push things in that direction unless you're getting some clear indicators of interest and receptivity from her. It's a very basic concept of empathy and communication that many men lack when dealing with women they consider lower and less conscious than themselves: Just because *you're* feeling a certain way toward someone does not mean *they* must be feeling the same way toward you.

A man *can* still be attracted to other women when he's in love with his soulmate. The difference is perspective. A pretty face is still a pretty face. A nice pair of tits will always be a nice pair of tits. It simply ceases to matter much to him. It becomes like a child's plaything, candy that would offer nothing of worth beyond a sugar rush followed by ickiness and lasting regret. How could the roundest, bounciest breasts in the world compare to the feeling my deepest love, my complementary soulmate, brings? Choosing anything over her would be like amputating part of myself—a partial suicide.

If you have a large breadth of experience in any domain, you know more about what is possible. You know more about yourself and your wants. Your choice matters more because it's an intentional narrowing down of a greater number of options, of things you know from experience could be better than what you happen to have or what the world would choose for you. You willingly reject them in favor of something incomparably superior that aligns most closely with who you are. Despite every other person I could be pursuing or every other place in the world I could be right now... I choose you. I choose this. There is nothing better in the universe for me than this.

I've had enough sex to know what is possible from it. Yet, I am burdened by the knowledge that I still don't have the type of sex I really want. I know that I need to be bonded to my soulmate and making love to her as often as possible. That's something I will never get tired of. It would be like getting tired of air. Just hold your breath for a minute. See if that whets your appetite again. See how long it takes for the desire to come back for the woman you love. Romantics know what they will find meaningful and enjoyable until the end of their life.

It seems a dubious claim to some men that they could ever move on from the desire to have sex with as many women as possible. Either cheating or the willful suppression of desires is inevitable, they think. It's betrayal waiting to happen unless these men psychologically neuter themselves. Avoiding betrayal is simply a matter of communication. It's about sticking to the agreements you make, both implicit and explicit, with your partner: consistency between behavior and expectation. It's not forcing yourself, inauthentically, to be a certain way. It's simply how you choose to act when you are fully self-expressed.

I will never be in denial of the part of myself that wants to have sex with hot young chicks. And because I don't pretend it doesn't exist, it doesn't have to be an issue for me or my monogamous partners. Everything is a matter of prioritization, and my highest priority is the woman I will love. Only men who deny who they are have to struggle with temptation. They project an image of who they think they are supposed to be in a relationship. They force themselves to pretend to be it, to live up to that image. You would only do that if you were unprepared to accept the reality of who you are.

There's an end to sexual curiosity so long as you allow yourself to fully explore what interests you. Then you start to realize you just might be ready to devote yourself to one particular path that stands out to you above the rest.

SETTLING FOR LESS THAN YOUR IDEAL

It's unsettling when a man settles for a woman who does not meet his personal standards for a soulmate. Of course, it's tragic, too, when a woman settles for a subpar man, but it's at least more understandable. She is subject to more social pressures to pair up before it is "too late," usually meaning before signs of aging show, before she loses her universal sexual appeal, and especially before she is too old to bear children. A man has no biological clock ticking down his fertile years, and it is more socially acceptable (often encouraged) for him to pair up with women much younger than him. With that luxury of extended choice, a man must be very weak or cowardly to give up the search for the woman he truly loves early. Even more tragic will it be if he chooses to have and raise children with a woman he is not totally aligned with, for his children will be unwitting victims of his lack of determination, too.

Refusing to settle for something less than what you want is not arrogance, entitlement, or even perfectionism. It is radical self-knowledge and dedication to the truth of who you are. Still,

I understand the temptation to give up the idealistic quest early for the sake of *any* form of companionship you can acquire if it eases the masculine burden even a little. A single man in society is like a stray dog. Ignoring the poor creature isn't the worst thing you can do to it. Giving it a home temporarily and then throwing it back out on the street again is far worse. In fact, it's downright monstrous. You will have given it the perspective of a warm, loving home and a place to belong that it may not ever acquire again. It will have greater capacity to suffer because of the perspective it now knows. Before, life was just life. Now, life will always be much worse than it can and should be. Now he knows what else he is capable of becoming, and it is so much more than what he is on his own.

It is incomprehensibly difficult for a man to return to the grayness of his void when once the world had color because of the connection the right woman brought to it. There will be a hole in his soul eating away at him. A shadow clinging. And no matter how happy he is in the moment, no matter how much life can offer him from its various other domains, he knows that other sources of pleasure or meaning will pass. It's the feeling that there's something you have to do, but you have no realistic way of accomplishing it. As smart as you are, as accomplished as you are, no matter how good you are at figuring other things out, you have no idea how this is ever going to work.

A romantic man needs a woman who needs him as much as he needs her. Someone who sees who he really is, sees the unique influence he has on her, realizes that no other man could ever measure up and have the same kind of effect. A woman is a place to a man, a whole world to belong in. Man is a seed, and woman is his soil. When social settings are such that romantic bonding between two compatible lovers cannot easily occur, the proactive man is caught between a rock and a hard place. He cannot do anything, but he also cannot do nothing. He has to work until he finds the one something that just might work. And when that, too, almost certainly fails to work, he must continue his search for the next something that stands any shot at being something. But it cannot just be companionship or a surrender to mediocrity.

When a woman is asked what she loves about her husband and responds with qualities that could be applied to any number of husbands, the attraction and chemistry are not personalized. "He has a good job. He doesn't drink too much. He treats me well and buys me nice things." It's the same when a man says he loves his wife because she's good to look at and takes care of the house and kids well. It's like trying to piece together an ideal candidate from a shopping list, even intricately imagining what the perfect man or woman would look like, smell like, talk like, and fuck like, gathering all the pieces from various sources and making an idol out of them. A man might even take physical features from his sexual partners and sculpt a hypothetical ideal woman who real women will never be able to live up to—though that won't stop them from trying if they have been conditioned to be desperate for his approval.

Some of the more superficial women I dated, the kind who liked me primarily because of how "interesting" I was, expressed to me how they wished they could combine me with their new boyfriends after we stopped dating. There were features I had that my replacements apparently lacked, and those poor women just couldn't get every box on their list checked. Though these women meant the comparison to be complimentary toward me, it made me feel bad for what the new masculine object in their life was in for by being with someone so shallow. By comparing their new partners to me instead of just experiencing them for who they were, they revealed the framework through which they assessed romantic connection. "What can I get out of this person? Is this the best deal in town to serve my needs? What can I learn from this piece of hardware so that I choose a better one next time I go shopping? How many more body parts can I fit in my Frankenstein's monster of a masculine partner?"

So many of the major complaints about modern relationships come down to the failure to live up to some cultural image of what role a partner is supposed to play in your life. When a woman is obsessed with the *idea* of marriage, it is to achieve the coveted social status of *being a married woman*. And if your marriage can be ruined because your wife doesn't have a hot dinner waiting for you when you come home, your marriage is not built on love and authentic compatibility. Domestic tasks should not define a romance. When a man and woman are in harmony, these mundane chores are hardly even noticed. It's just each unit of a partnership doing what they perceive to be what will best aid their shared goals. Should a man open doors for a woman? Only if it is more in his nature than hers to do so. If it's more energy efficient, in the same way that we open doors for a stranger whose hands are occupied. It would be a greater inconvenience for them to try to open it on their own than with the help of someone, even a stranger, who can do so relatively easily. It's a basic principle of symbiosis in economy and ecology. Each person does what they are best suited to do. When a man offers to carry something heavy or open a stubborn pickle jar for a woman, it should be because he is stronger and it is less of a burden for him to do so. The principle is stronger person vs. weaker person, not male vs. female.

Why do we expect that men should pay for things for women? Because, historically, it has been easier for men to be more economically successful than women. That's a fault in the development of civilization, not something inherent to the masculine and feminine dichotomy. That fault has already all but disappeared in the developed world and is rapidly doing so almost everywhere else. Automatically assuming that because someone is a woman, a man must open the door, lift the heavy thing, or pay for dinner for her because she is incapable of doing so on her own or the burden would be inordinately difficult is one of the most sexist and demeaning generalizations I can imagine.

It is creating more problems than necessary. A problem is something you have to think about in order to solve. Cooking is a problem that needs to be solved. Food preparation takes time, skill, and effort. And some people are much better at it or enjoy it much more than others. It will be stressful for some people and fulfilling for others. So when should a woman cook for a man? When it is more in her nature than his to do so. She should do that either if she enjoys it more or she is better at it and the two agree upon it as the optimal arrangement between them. To love and support someone is not to enable their infantilization. It's to empower them as much as possible with your strengths. When two people can sustainably reciprocate the strengths of their gendered differences toward each other, you have relationship harmony.

Love does not have to mean self-sacrifice—worsening yourself to make the other person better or expecting them to do the same for your sake. When you spend money on something that will make your life better, you're losing money, but you're getting something back in return that's better than the money you spent. By giving you what you want, I also get what I want, more than I could get on my own. By giving me what I want, you also get more of what you want. We're both always improving because of each other. Two plus two now equals five, and the whole becomes greater than the sum of the parts.

RECOGNIZING YOU ARE IN LOVE (OR THAT A MAN IS IN LOVE WITH YOU)

Falling in love, genuine love, with another person whose existence is uniquely capable of elevating you to that state and keeping you there feels akin to suddenly waking from a dream that had gone on so long that you forgot it was not real. There is now so much more to reality, and you don't know what to do with it all. You are so much more than you were before. Maybe this is the only thing that was ever real. To stay in this love requires the acceptance of a state which, by all previous known laws, should not be able to exist.

In those rare, perfect circumstances, we stop even considering how things could ever be better. That is the closest to heaven on earth we can get to if we can find a sustainable source of experience that nullifies our desire to try to improve upon it or seek something better. It is our only way to live completely in the present, such that we stop lamenting how things could have happened differently in the past or planning how they ought to go in the future. This, right here and now, is all I could ever want. *You*, my dear, are all I could ever want. A man with his soulmate cannot imagine that things can or should be any better than they are. He is, at last, free from his eternal search for *something* and the pursuit of greater meaning. That is the effect of a great work of art, too. That is what overwhelming beauty feels like—like it is the entire universe, and nothing outside it matters for at least as long as you are blessed enough to be able to experience it.

It's how I've always pictured a marriage should go. A husband and wife should be profoundly grateful every day that somehow, out of the infinite chance and chaos that make up social interaction, they managed to find one another, build a sustainable bond, and experience the optimal arrangement of being together.

No matter what momentary problems arise, they should never stop appreciating the fact that they won the romantic lottery and somehow beat probability by having each other in their lives. Their pairing should be seen as a miracle worth celebrating every day that it endures. That's a rational concept of marriage that transcends the social or religious notion it has become. Conscious commitment to one person is not a sacrifice if you are mature and know what you want. It is complete dedication to your ideals, the principle of who you are.

Some believe that falling in love shouldn't be all that exciting, that it should be calm. But I know how stimulating it can be to realize how compatible you are with someone, which is different from the shallower, higher-energy type of excitement you get from just being attracted to them. More than anything, it is relieving. Each time, I have found myself asking, "Is this it? Are the trials finally over? Do I get to rest now?" Falling in love feels a bit like dying, and I mean that in the best possible way. The feeling remains well after excitement has faded.

It can even be surreal if you are unfamiliar with the experience. You might need to have experienced both the real thing and its crude imitators a few times to be sure of what is happening. You very quickly find yourself forgetting whatever little imperfections might have otherwise prevented you from being fully attracted to, invested in, and bonded with someone when all the right elements are a match. We can even feel like we have known someone our whole lives after only a short time of being in love with them. We are identifying the immortal principle that defines them. That's as good a concept of a soul as I've ever heard. You don't need to have been there for years at their side to get an accurate conception of who they have been and how they will act, so long as they are honest and sufficiently self-expressed.

A signature indicator of romantic love is the creative motivation and potential it activates in men. That's why we expect love songs, poetry, and other forms of artistic expression to germinate from it. It's a demonstration, a sort of proof of the effect a woman is having on a man. "Prove you love me by showing me the transformative effect my presence in your life has had on you. What can you do now that you would not have been able to do without me?" Do you know how I knew I was beginning to fall in love the last time it happened? It was in the way the trees looked more detailed and beautiful to me on the drive home one day. That's how it happens. It's not a feeling contained to the woman or anything I directly associate with her. My perception of the world deepens because her influence allows me access to parts of myself that are normally buried.

For most young women, it's not hard to attract at least some, if not most, men in a superficial way. They will initiate innocent conversations in the hopes that the discourse might turn flirtatious. They will throw every cheesy pickup line in the book at them if there's a chance it might endear them. They will buy them drinks, thinking that it means they now owe them a minute of their attention. Some will even insist that they love them, that they can't stop thinking about them, or that they're the most beautiful woman they've ever seen. After a while, women just expect it as a byproduct of their existence. Infatuation like this is easy and frequently mistaken for love. We get preoccupied with it because it is the most visible symptom of romance.

Here is what I would ask my daughter about any boy she was dating who professed to feel strongly about her: "Do you see a man become a better, more fully expressed version of himself around you as a consequence of your influence? Do you see that he cannot pull his heart away from you because you bring peace to his life and activate his potential? Do you make all the beauty in the universe come alive for him, such that your influence lingers on him like a scent even when you are gone? Are you like the sun to him, the origin of light and warmth that all life on Earth reveres, the source of all his superpowers?"[33] That is how a man who wholly loves you will react to the fact of your existence. It is a holistic type of love. You could do nothing to change it because it is integral to who you both are, the natural chemical reaction of your mixing.

Love can only be as certain as anything else can ever be. Everything you think ever happens is only your best guess at what the hell is going on. That being said, there are some things we can be pretty sure about, things like the sunrise and the laws of physics. And maybe true love is one of those things. Brian Wilson and The Beach Boys sang that though it's possible he may not always love you, you'd never need to doubt his feelings so long as there were still stars in the sky above you. Consider how simultaneously grounded and pie-in-the-sky this sentiment is. We cannot be 100% certain about our everlasting love, but we can be as sure as humanly possible—as sure as one can be about the stars in the sky continuing to shine. As sure as the laws of physics and observable astronomical events with thousands of years of recorded history. As sure as the heavens themselves. "Until reality as we know it fundamentally breaks, you can be sure of how I feel about you."

I don't have to be 100% sure about the woman I love before I marry her; I only have to be sure enough to bet the rest of

---

33 *The yellow sun of Earth's solar system plays both a literal and metaphorical role in activating the signature array of powers held by the character Superman. He does not manifest his various superpowers until under the influence of our sun. Just as with the love of the right woman in his life, he is only a man, not "super," without the sun's constant light and warmth.*

my life on it. Love is a risk I am willing to lose everything for, willing even to die for. Logically, I should be willing to dedicate the rest of my life to its implementation.

If you asked most people how they know they love their partner, they'd talk largely about an emotion they are presently experiencing. The strength of that emotion is so strong, in this moment, that they assume that it can never change. But the fact that you feel very strongly right now does not necessarily mean anything about what you will feel tomorrow or ten or more years from now. Many marriages that start as strongly as possible still end in divorce (or worse: lifelong romantic unfulfillment).

When I'm sure that I am in love with a woman, it's never just because I feel strongly about her or that she has qualities I revere and am attracted to. It's the intensity of that feeling combined with radical self-knowledge and experience in the domain of romance. I know with a high degree of confidence what kind of person I am, including what type of romantic interaction I find sustainably meaningful, engaging, and attractive. This even includes sureness of sustainable physical attraction. Can I picture this person getting old and ugly? Do I know that I will still be physically attracted to them even under the worst conditions? Yes. I know what I find attractive, what kind of person I want to talk to, spend my time around, and make love to for the rest of my life.

To fall in love with someone is to fall in love with the principle of who they are. Within the scope of that principle exists the potential for their best and worst, their highest virtues and lowest vices. When you love the principle, you see what else they could and ought to become, even when they are showing you their worst parts. Likewise, you remain intimately aware of the worst they could be even when they are treating you well. The universal human struggle lies in trying to embody the best of ourselves in circumstances that don't always make it easy. The burden is greatly alleviated by the support of a complementary partner who sees who you are aiming to be.

Of course, all this is assuming that *both* halves of the partnership equation are of a similar nature *and* fully self-expressed in that nature. Your relationship will still be doomed if you misjudge the nature of the person you are bonding with or there are obstacles to them fully embodying it.

CHAPTER 6

Watching the Women
You Love Die

> *"There is no worse evil than a bad woman, and nothing has ever been produced better than a good one."*
>
> — Euripides

I have discussed what the worst, most immature, suppressive, and coercive men have done to women. But here now comes a necessary warning for romantic men, too. We underestimate a woman's ability to destroy us with the power we give her. We trust that she will naturally only do beautiful things with it because we perceive her as a purely beautiful creature.

An insecure woman seeks power over men through emotional manipulation. She plants dreams in men's heads about a future they desire, a future where all that color and beauty will be theirs and they will never have to return to their monochrome ugliness. She masters the art of telling men exactly what they want to hear, showing obvious signs of interest and leading them on with glimmers of hope and progress. Such women are playing with powerful, dangerous forces and do not take responsibility for their influence, treating men like ravenous animals only to the degree it benefits them and then disregarding them when it does not. There is not enough supply to meet the demand they cultivate for their social benefit. Most men will be doomed to denial from what they pursue.

Already, many women will rise to arms defending these behaviors as essential parts of their femininity, of "just being a woman." Men, too, make the same mistake of accepting this toxicity as an expression of womanhood. It's indicative of the systemic problem we are still facing: that women and men often still see the worst aspects of their undeveloped natures as goals to strive for, characteristics that define them and should be cherished and compensated for. Being a crass and horny brute is not what makes you a man, but you will continue to be that way so long as you have been conditioned to take the easy path of your masculine development. It is the same with being a manipulative bitch for women.

It begins with an innocent expectation we breed into women: special treatment for being a woman—merit preceding character or action. Taken as a lifelong absolute, it breeds an abominable sense of entitlement. She comes to accept that men, and even the world itself, are resources to serve her. She is a trophy to be won—and man is a machine built to win her if he is up to it. The whole of the cosmos should bend to her majesty as a royal or even divine feminine being. She is a non-volitional vessel for cultivating appreciation. You'll see hints in her everyday behavior, but you might never dream of how far she can take it under the most extreme circumstances. Perhaps they are only unfortunate aberrations upon a deep and beautiful soul. She has kept it under control around you, to show you enough of what you want to see in her, what she *needs* you to see in her to get what she needs from you. You suspend your disbelief because it is so goddamn attractive compared to the alternative, the world you knew without her influence.

Eventually, there will come a switch: a dramatic change in personality, priorities, or working terms of the romance, and you will wonder if you even knew this person at all because how they behave now is incompatible with the person they were before. Perhaps you are not dealing with a person at all anymore but a machine, a psychological program that bends people and circumstances to support the story it tells about itself. It's a survival mechanism in a pretty package. The beautiful woman you knew, the one you loved, perhaps even your soulmate, has died. Something uglier has taken her place.

THE FEMININE MINEFIELD

A bond between people is a shared psychological structure. Expectations and understanding create the feeling of knowing and being known. But even the strongest bonds can be threatened if either party is subject to destructive outbursts that threaten everything built. It is like stepping on a landmine. Usually, you have no reason to think the terrain you are traversing might be dangerous and that you need to keep your guard up. You step the same way you've stepped a million times before, and—BOOM— the entire structure is now in ruins. It's impossible to determine where the ever-moving line is until after it's been crossed. I can't tell you how many times I have inadvertently enraged a woman who was otherwise very fond of me by doing nothing different than usual. And then, without warning and for reasons I can never discern ahead of time, my behavior sets off an explosive reaction. Something that should not have been taken seriously is, then, in that moment, the most serious thing in the world.

If femininity is oriented around experience, whatever is happening in any given moment is what's most real and important. Any prior conception is less valid than what's happening right now. Women, once mistreated (and who among them hasn't been?), can be conditioned into believing they are under constant threat. They wear their emotions like armor to deflect attempts to get inside and harm them. There is a crucial period where they must decide what the real and relevant truth is, especially when feelings conflict with knowledge and memories. Experience goes to war with conception, the internal feminine versus the internal masculine. A woman who's self-aware and embodied in femininity knows she can be prone to chaos caused by how she happens to feel. She's naturally attracted to a man who is the opposite of that: stable and consistent. She knows what to expect from him: discipline over body and mind. When destructive force is required, he aims his violence away from her and toward potential threats.

A man can never be a tornado, a hurricane, or any form of out-of-control, indiscriminate force. His consciousness is unidirectional. A hammer. A laser. A lightsaber: a concentrated beam of energy that only extends to a determined length, activated as long as needed and deactivated when not. The man who punches holes in drywall because his favorite sports team lost or he's had a stressful day is signaling that he cannot control himself or tolerate much stimulation. If a woman ever has to worry that he can physically harm her in a heated moment, even accidentally, it means he has done a poor job showing that he's in control of himself. If she has to worry that he will lose himself in sexual passion and prematurely ejaculate, he is putting her at risk of unwanted pregnancy because his body can't handle the intensity. She needs to feel that he is the rock upon which she is safe to express her chaotic self.

But a tornadoed woman makes a major mistake when she aims her chaos *at* the man who loves her, the person most bonded to her, just because she feels safest with him. She dare not display this side of herself to the rest of the world. It's like how a child sees their parents as obligated to love and support them. Mom and dad are invincible; so too should be the man in a woman's life, she tells herself. A mature woman has healthier ways of expressing her chaos and fire. She does not have to treat her man like a bombproof shelter. She is never willing to threaten their relationship and all the trust and comfort built with her partner. A bad mood or momentary offense is never more important than the structure of their bond. Damage and offense of various types are inevitable. A relationship must strengthen through them, even due to them, like muscles repairing themselves to a stronger state after the stress of a good workout. The bond between soulmates must be antifragile.[34]

Solving an emotional crisis with your partner strengthens your bond. Every crisis is an opportunity. As conflict is inevitable, what matters is how you dedicate yourselves to responding to it. When the impulse in the face of conflict is to move further apart, the relationship is unsustainable. When the impulse in the face of conflict is the move closer together, it will grow stronger the longer it lasts. But if the default response to stress is to shut off communication, as it most often is between couples, it makes conflict impossible to resolve. It may take time

---

34 *Antifragility is a concept developed by Nassim Nicholas Taleb in his book Antifragile (Penguin Books, 2012). Antifragile systems are those that strengthen and improve through shocks, stress, disorder, and volatility because they adapt and evolve from the experience.*

to process everything, to not want to jump into discussion right away because the process is too taxing. But even during that time, you maintain the awareness that the goal is to improve communication, closeness, trust, and the structure of the bond.

THE LOVE OF A BAD WOMAN

Tamsin, an outwardly posh but inwardly insecure, ultra-modern London girl, was what most men would consider to be the most conventionally attractive girl I was ever in a real relationship with. And, *boy*, did she know it. Early on, I warned her, "If you're looking for someone who is going to spend a lot of money on you, spoil you, and treat you like a princess, there are plenty of guys who would love to do that for you. But I am not that guy. I will *never* be that guy." Though she protested otherwise, there was an unspoken standard she carried with her about how I should be treating her, and she was perpetually disappointed with me for failing to live up to it. I was the first man in her life to value her for her mind and capabilities instead of her appearance, which contradicted every bit of social reinforcement she had received as a beautiful object since she was the prettiest little girl around and the apple of her parents' eyes.

Though it was her appearance that captured my attention when we first met, it was something else about her that made her unignorable to me. She was sharp and complex inside in ways that no one else had ever noticed about her or encouraged her to develop until I came along. I recognized her as similar to me in many ways, but I also saw that she had never learned to take responsibility for her actions and influence. Born into the body of an attractive woman, she had been given far more social leeway for self-indulgent, manipulative behavior. I also thought that Tamsin was the first woman who might have the potential to understand me the way I always wanted to be understood by a woman. That ended up being the foundation of our entire relationship: hope for her potential, hope for the woman I foresaw she would one day turn into when she was ready.

Tamsin's unhealthy paradigm of romance and expected gender roles was clear from the start. She always had to test me, to see what efforts I would take to impress her. Almost everywhere she went, men checked her out or flirted with her, and she usually allowed them to do so right in front of me. This was the first in what became a series of increasingly dismissive behaviors. The first time we went traveling together, she would leave me alone in our hotel room to go sightseeing alone. In Hampstead Heath, I always found her walking several paces ahead instead of next to me, like she was traveling alone in her mind, and I was just some financer and bellhop tagging along. On the numerous occasions I told her that I was ready to leave her over her repeated disregard for me, she broke down crying and promised to start treating me better. This defined our dynamic for years: wild back-and-forths between devotion when she felt threatened and disregard once she was no longer in danger of being abandoned.

It's ironic that Tamsin was the only woman I've ever had trouble performing sexually with when you consider how badly other men wanted to fuck her. Even though I found her physically attractive, I almost totally lost the ability to view her in an intimate way. With every other woman, once a base level of attraction and comfort had been established, sex was mostly a matter of gradually moving our bodies closer together. The rest took care of itself. But without emotional comfort, nothing about the way she looked mattered to me. I couldn't be vulnerable with her. Sex was some kind of performance I was obligated to put on for her, to show her how grateful I should have been to have the opportunity to experience her naked body the way so many other men wanted to, creating a market demand that she mistook for interpersonal chemistry. To her, sex was a social concept, a dominance game—a form of currency or incentive structure. She couldn't understand that the one man in the world who didn't want to sleep with her, her boyfriend, had standards that went beyond merely thinking she looked good naked, that he required emotional vulnerability.

The day she spontaneously broke up with me, I didn't fight it. I wasn't even surprised. It seemed inevitable, so I let it happen. I knew the idealist in me was never going to give up on her enough to end things with her, not so long as it saw potential for things to get better. Frankly, I felt relieved that it was finally over, and I was free from the pressure of being expected to live up to her fantasies about what a man was supposed to be. But when she saw how easy it was for me to move on and start dating again when she had been expecting that I'd come crawling back, her chronic fear of abandonment kicked into overdrive. The break-up hadn't been meant to be taken seriously by me. It was only a manipulative tactic to see how hard I'd work to keep her in my life. As soon as I told her I was getting romantically involved with another woman, a fact I made sure to inform her of so there would be no traumatic surprises later on, the same old charade ensued to stop me. Tears. Panic. Pleading that we could still be together and that she'd do anything to change for me. Tale as old as time, a pattern that has shown up in every manipulative relationship ever. Maybe this time will be different. Maybe they've finally learned how to treat me.

When I found out Tamsin had cheated on me after we got back together, I also should not have been surprised. It should not have affected me at all, in the same way her sudden desire to end our relationship had not. But it did, and she seemed completely oblivious as to why. For only the briefest moment of forced self-realization, she admitted to feeling like a monster because of what she had done. "I *understand*, intellectually, that you are right and I betrayed you. But I still *feel* like I am right," she confessed in a fleeting moment of self-awareness and conceptual clarity. There was that smart girl I fell in love with, the one with a world of undeveloped potential inside her, briefly peeking out from underneath the shadow that had taken over her behavior, letting the virtue of accurate conception have the smallest of voices in a sea of chaotic self-indulgent feeling. And in the depths of the destruction she caused our bond, somehow, still, she could not understand why I was not comfortable enough with her to make love to her—like it was still some service I was obligated to perform for her under the worst and least intimate of possible conditions. In her mind, the jealousy of knowing she had been with another man should have spurned territorial lust from me over her body, an object I was supposed to be possessive over as its rightful owner.

It's deeply hurtful to realize that someone who vowed to be faithful to you has broken that trust. Beyond jealousy, what stays is the unsettling realization that you have to question everything you thought you knew about this person, every idea you had of who they are. Perhaps you never knew them at all. The structure of your psychological bond is in shambles. The hardest fact to integrate was that I was in love with someone who could do one of the worst things possible to someone who loves them and show no remorse, instantly wiping the nature of her actions from her consciousness. How bad a judge of character was I that I could be so deeply invested in someone willing to treat me so poorly? I had to confront the weakness in myself that put me in this position: I could not trust my standard for whom to apply my powerful romantic nature to. Perhaps my entire cosmic worldview was fundamentally wrong. Perhaps I did not live in an ordered universe at all, but one of chaos and terrors beyond my wildest imaginings.

Tamsin's problematic behavior had been obvious from the start. I was never blind to it. I only had faith that she'd outgrow it. There was always that little spark of hope that she wouldn't do what she was destined to do, that she would learn and grow instead. The idealist always sees the best in people, always sees what they are hypothetically capable of, always wants to do whatever they can to help them embody it. They don't see that you cannot fix or save a person who has a broken internal model about themselves. They will use your greatest strengths, your compassion and romantic idealism, against you. You cannot negotiate reality with someone who has embraced delusion about who they are and the world they live in. Since love is built on shared identification, one partner's struggles, pain, and downfall should also be felt by the other. Hurting the person you love should be the same as harming yourself.

I know that I would never cheat on a woman. Not because I couldn't feel tempted to. Not because I could never find other women attractive while in a committed relationship. If I felt the urge to cheat, I would take it as a sign that there was something seriously wrong with my relationship. I would then make it my priority to either resolve the issue or end the partnership as fairly as possible. I would communicate this clearly with my partner so she would know what to expect from me. Only then would I pursue someone else romantically. Only then would it *not* be cheating. I am so dedicated to this ideal that I have gone out of my way to inform ex-girlfriends after we broke up of new romantic developments in my life before acting on them as a courtesy to them and whatever lingering expectations they might have had toward me so that they could align as closely as possible with the new reality we were now living in.

Jealousy is a great early warning system. If you ever have to feel jealous in a relationship, it's a clear sign that something isn't right. If you ever feel tempted to try to make your partner feel jealous, take a good long look in the mirror and think about why you are considering that this manipulative tactic is the best way to get something you want from someone you're supposed to see as an extension of yourself. Jealousy is no more a good way to keep a relationship exciting than chest pain is to remind you to keep your heart healthy.

The stereotypical reason men cheat on women has much more to do with momentary indulgence in lust than some kind of moral justification about empowerment. A cheating man typically knows that what he's doing is wrong, but he does it anyway because he is weak and has not fully integrated his rampant sexual curiosity. He remains ashamed of his indulgence in momentary weakness and hides his actions from his partner because of it. When a woman cheats, she is more likely to have somehow concocted the story that what she's doing is perfectly justified, even empowering. She selects memories that support her chosen course of action, remembering all the times her partner has ever done anything bad to her and forgetting all the times he's ever done anything good.

That's the path to corrupted personal empowerment Tamsin took, all the while letting the world confirm for her that she only did what she needed to do to feel like the woman she wanted to be. A world that prioritizes appearance and instant gratification will never hold beautiful women accountable for their actions. To it, they are still not fully volitional agents, not fully adult humans, but decorations fulfilling a function.

FEMININE AMNESIA

An undercooked feminine mind is a hopelessly flighty thing, barely able to hold on to long-term memories and associations. It is subject to whatever it happens to be feeling, even without understanding why it feels that way. It rejects introspection and conscious rationalization because concepts about experiences fall under the domain of masculinity. When emotions go to war with understanding, the mind has to recollect events selectively. A woman then edits her working memory like a writer edits a working draft, cutting out anything that doesn't support how she's currently feeling about how the story should go or has gone. Of course, we all filter and interpret. But the degree to which and the way it happens with upset women, and the fact that it shifts with whatever mood they're in, is something distinct from the masculine experience. Something about the feminine temperament and its orientation around current states makes them more susceptible to emotion overriding cognitive understanding.

I have driven hours to see women just to learn that they had decided not to see me as planned but didn't feel it pertinent to inform me ahead of time. I have made plans to attend events with women months in advance, reminding them all along the way up to the impending date, only for them not to show up and seemingly not understand why I expected them to or why it would upset me so much that they didn't. I have had women keep cars I paid for without my permission. I have invested thousands of dollars of capital into professional projects to support women I loved who later decided that my investments were really just donations all along. In all these cases and more, the immature women I was dealing with seemed to be in complete denial of the facts of their own behavior. At their moment of upset, the agreements made and expectations previously set simply didn't *feel* real to them anymore. Thus, it was as though they had never been real at all.

The recurring justification for toxic femininity is personal empowerment and self-expression. You'll hear a thousand forms of it: a woman who cheats on her partner because it is "just what she needs to do to feel beautiful" or "like a sexually fulfilled woman." Abandoning plans and agreements because they don't "serve how she feels" anymore. These irresponsible girlboss moments are socially celebrated. The masculine mind, meanwhile, relies on a memory of things, including patterns of action and agreements held between parties, to interpret how it should feel and act. Woman more readily casts herself beyond those ordered confines into randomness and chaos without justification. That's why undeveloped women can change their minds on a dime, even about the most important things in the world. They can forget years of personal history and expectations when the responsibility of keeping them becomes too much for her emotions.

An actual justification for the way the amnesiac woman feels will only be invented later, in retrospect. Memories will morph to align with a narrative that makes her chaotic behavior seem natural, reasonable, necessary, and even empowering. It's shocking how quickly one's personal history can be forgotten and replaced by something that might be the opposite of what actually occurred. Even in the age of ample records for digital communication, such as text, recorded voice, and video, there is little to stop an unbridled mind from distorting facts with dissociative ad hoc explanations.

How can you trust someone once you know they are capable of maintaining a straight face while they distort reality so much? You cannot share a conception of reality with someone who has no consistent memory of events. You cannot be intimate with someone who cannot self-reflect, as there is no self to bond with. It's perpetual miscommunication between cognition and reality.

A highly feminine woman needs to be self-aware enough to know that she has this weakness, that she sometimes cannot trust her own selected memories and first interpretation of events, especially when she is feeling unsafe. If she treats this tendency like it's a healthy aspect of femininity or something to be proud of, she will justify the worst things one person can do to another.

The most offensive thing you can do to a woman caught in such a state of non-reality is to remind her of the facts and hold her accountable to the truth. Accountability feels like dying to her because you are attacking her with a parallel reality that, if deeply and fairly considered, stands to threaten everything she has accepted about the person she thinks she is. You are never just arguing one event, one point of data, or one fact. You are arguing the nature of her existence. That's why confronting the truth feels like dying to a liar. It's very easy for her then to move from a state of indifference about the truth to one of active antagonism against it. Anyone who acts as an ambassador of the truth becomes her enemy—someone she is willing to destroy to avoid being reminded of accountability. That is how you see a beautiful woman you knew seem to be overtaken by some kind of unrecognizable devil driven wholly by vitriol. She, the structure of her identity, dies when she becomes the worst possible version of herself by indulging wholly in all her vices and murdering the highest potential she was once hypothetically capable of.

What's too painful to remember we simply choose to forget, so sang Barbara.

In the interest of reasonable self-defense and not wasting years of our lives determining the truth about a woman's character, there must be clear dealbreakers in place when evaluating her behavior. There must be reliable tests of character and action that, if failed, reveal the undeniable truth about the woman you are intimately connected to. If you ever realize that you would never, in a million years and at your worst moments, treat the woman you love the way she is treating you, you will have also realized that you are occupying fundamentally different roles in each other's lives, telling different stories and playing different games, *living in different realities.*

Even getting cheated on was not, in and of itself, a dealbreaker for me. As soon as I was confronted with the truth of what Tamsin, the woman I loved, had done, I knew that I would have been willing to work through it with her. The dealbreaker (or Diehlbreaker in this case) was the way she confessed this crime to me, followed by her distorted assessment of her own behavior. If she had come to me saying how sorry she was for the mistake she had made, I know that I could have forgiven her. We could have put the long work into recovering from the injury she had brought to the structure of our bond. That she was so dismissive proved that a point of no return had been reached. She had shown who she was at her core: a fundamentally *bad person* who either did not care about treating the people who loved her rightly or was incapable of figuring out how to do so.

In the years after I stopped communicating with Tamsin, I became wary that I might have allowed time and grief to distort my perception of her character. It's all too easy to demonize someone once you know the evil they are capable of and forget all the good that coexisted with it. I never tried to deny that there were good times and moments of genuine connection between us despite the pain she had caused me. Maybe she had grown as a person since then. Instead, I learned that the very opposite had occurred. A mere few years after the incident that changed my life forever, she displayed no knowledge that she had even cheated on me at all. I know that when it happened, she was not in denial of the physical reality of what she had done—only the moral interpretation. She was not afraid to call it cheating but argued that it did not really matter. Somehow in the time since then, she had managed to overwrite that information in her mind and had no idea what she had done to me. One of the most painful events of my life was not even noteworthy enough to her to remember doing.

What a terrifying reality to consider.

My standard with women now is simple but absolute: If someone has had the opportunity to honestly self-reflect on their actions and still shows no remorse or repentance for a mistake made under the influence of insecure emotions, I cannot associate with them. They have chosen a distorted version of reality to align themselves with, and we are not sharing the same universe anymore. If they can justify even seemingly small acts of dishonesty or violated expectations, there's no way to be sure they won't do the same when it really matters after years have been invested into building our bond. Even the smallest acknowledgment of indiscretion on their part might be enough to restore the strength of the bond and avoid structural collapse.

THE ROMANTIC CULTURE WAR

There is one more tragic consequence of man's systemic negation of feminine agency in attempts to contain her purity and innocence. A culturally restricted woman is attracted to a free man because he brings a bit of his freedom to her. Love becomes a battle between your freedom and her unfreedom. On one side of the fight lies everything the two of you could ever want from the experience of one another. On the other are all the insecurities about pursuing that ambition and the pressure to conform to expectations for how her life should go.

It's no coincidence that this battle is often what classic love stories depict and why we love them. They present a mythological truth about this aspect of the human experience. The classic love story goes: A rogue man operating outside of society's norms and customs catches the attention of a woman (often a literal princess) entrenched in a position of higher status and comfort. His task is to inspire her through his masculine heroism and romantic gestures to open her heart to the possibility of stepping away from the restrictive world she knows. He awakens the romantic spirit within her. Her survival and comfort depend on evaluation from her social order, but he has no such restrictions because he is independent. He lives outside the system on his own terms. She is attracted to him because she longs for a sense of the freedom he has built for himself. Following that attraction would require her to give up everything the world has offered her on a silver platter.

In Disney's *Aladdin*, restricted Princess Jasmine is instantly drawn to and eventually falls in love with local "street rat," Aladdin. She rejects her father, the sultan's, attempts to wed her to a proper prince, as preordained by her social role, instead choosing the clever and caring man of action. He shows her a whole new world, a whole new way of being, and frees her from her bonds, ultimately changing the order of the society around them.

"Tell me, princess. Now, when did you last let your heart decide?"

— Aladdin to Princess Jasmine, *Aladdin*

In the *Star Wars* original trilogy, Princess Leia is not confined by societal restrictions in the same way as conventional princesses.

She's a headstrong leader in a rebellion against an evil empire. Still, she has to learn to open her heart and embrace her femininity by accepting her attraction to scoundrel smuggler with a heart of gold Han Solo, despite initially butting heads with him. Her demeanor is notably softer and more at peace by the final film as a result of loving him.

"You like me because I'm a scoundrel. There aren't enough scoundrels in your life."

— Han Solo to Princess Leia,
Star Wars Episode V: The Empire Strikes Back

Baz Luhrmann's *Moulin Rouge!* tells of Christian, a young English writer and quintessential romantic idealist who falls in love with the star courtesan Satine at the famous Moulin Rouge cabaret. Satine's social identity as the highest-class prostitute for Paris' wealthy and elite forces certain restrictions on her, including her insistence that love is a delusion and dangerous to indulge in—until, against all odds and precedent, she falls for the penniless bohemian and proves willing to sacrifice everything about her posh lifestyle and the overwhelming expectations thrust upon her to pursue it. She, at last, accepts that fundamental virtues like freedom, beauty, truth, and love matter more than staying safe in the control of established structures that resist the revolution of human expression, wholly and earnestly captured in her grand public declaration of her forbidden love for Christian in the final moments of her life.

> *"A life without love? That's terrible!"*
> *"No, being on the street, that's terrible."*
> *"No! Love is like oxygen! Love is a many splendored thing!*
> *Love lifts us up where we belong! All you need is love!"*
> — Christian and Satine, *Moulin Rouge!*

The male romantic rival in such stories is most often represented by a prince or shallow man of similarly high social stature. Rather than the strict lack of material wealth, it's the social identity of the rogue that conflicts with that of the princess. A man who makes or spends money in an unconventional way can still be seen as a threat to the established order. Even a wealthy rogue challenges his princess' presuppositions about who she is and the world she lives in. The culturally condoned romantic rival represents the easier choice to surrender romantic ambition for social comfort, to give up on heroic exploration and self-expression and stay safe in the limitations one knows.

It might seem as though the fact that the lovers come from different worlds means they cannot ever be together. That's why this timeless pairing scares so many. It's much easier to settle for someone more obvious, someone from "their world" who is already a fit for how they know how to live. Seeking out an identical partner requires almost no effort. Married life will be virtually identical to the single life that preceded it. But the romantic man seeks the woman who will complement and complete him, not merely validate the life he has made for himself.

The happy ending to this story is that our rogue wins the trust of his princess and breaks her out of her social prison. She, meanwhile, brings him into her stability. They take the best from each other and accomplish what seemed impossible. And they live "happily ever after" in glory that reshapes the world around them. The sad ending is that the woman's fear of losing the comfort of good social standing leads her to reject her true love suitor. She succumbs to the inertia and entropy of her environment. At the moment of surrender, she will undergo a shift to pretending she holds no feelings at all until she forces herself to forget them completely due to the trauma they cause her.

The only way to be together is to build a new world that they can both be part of, one composed of their respective strengths and operating under better, emergent rules. Their bonding goes so far as to be physically embodied by the creation of new life that is half of each of them. Children are the first native inhabitants of the whole new world they create out of love for one another—love that conquers the borders and distance put in place by culture and tradition.

Societies built on order and tradition are particularly threatened by romantic self-expression. Fear and shame keep the population in line. Blossoming love among the idealistic youth is dangerous because it is as powerful as it is unpredictable. It lessens the control of those in power. It's why parents arrange marriages for their sons and daughters with "safe" partners who follow the expectations of their culture and won't threaten the influence they have over their offspring. It will be almost impossible for women, in particular, to make radical changes once they cement themselves into the role their families, societies, and husbands expect of them.

> *"They fear love because it creates a world they can't control."*
>
> — Winston Smith, *1984* by George Orwell
> (Secker & Warburg, 1949)

Despite my many opportunities at love and lifelong romantic ambition, Zehra is the only woman I have ever seriously attempted to marry and spend my life with. The day I proposed to her, I told her, "I don't have many firsts left. But you're the first girl I've ever asked to marry me. And I hope the only one." That's the incredible ideal she lived up to in my eyes. That's how at peace I became by the fact of her existence and proximity to her being. It was remarkably easy to recognize that what I felt with her was the mythical feeling I had been looking for in every romantic encounter up to then. By asking her to spend the rest of her life with me, I was making a claim to her and the universe: that I was sure enough of my love and our natural compatibility to dedicate the rest of my life to it. I was removing all ambiguity and uncertainty for her. Until then, she couldn't be certain of the security of being with me. I offered her the most certainty humanly possible: a lifetime guarantee. But I could not be certain that she'd reciprocate. That risk, my willingness to act without certainty of success, is what made it romantic. That's why it's usually the man proposing marriage or even just initiating flirtation, courtship, and sex. He is better equipped to bear failure, to take damage and survive and grow from it. Masculinity is forged in fire. More often than not, for romantic men, women are that fire. He grows stronger, more self-aware, and more committed to his ideals if he can survive and integrate each disappointment.

Despite thinking of herself as a hopeless romantic, Zehra had spent her life beholden to her restrictive Turkish upbringing. No man before me had ever managed to activate her hidden romantic side that stood in direct contrast to how she had been conditioned to think about the traditional role of a man in her life. Her culture forbade women from making their own choices without parental oversight and strict adherence to ancient courtship norms. The first time I confessed my romantic feelings and told her the profound effect she was having on me, she confessed that she had always dreamed of having someone express such things about her. I justified my declaration of love in the simplest of ways: "When I'm with you, I am happy. I finally feel like I belong in the universe. What more do I need to know?" The first time we kissed, her very first kiss of all at the late age of 27, she told me she couldn't imagine the night having possibly gone any better or aligning more closely with the hopeless romanticism she gleaned by watching Western movies in which such dramatic scenes that clashed with her constrained emotional upbringing were depicted. It was like a fairy tale come true—something previously considered impossible but now, somehow, miraculously happening to her.

Our natural chemistry in every domain was obvious, except for one clear outlier: cultural expectations about life and love. In her society, I was an outsider in a traditional society that was heavily prejudiced against foreigners and foreign ways of doing things. It was ironic. One of the reasons she was drawn to me was that she saw me as an opportunity to branch out from the restrictions of her culture and explore the romantic parts of herself it had never allowed her to. And now, it was the very same restrictions that she had taken so much risk to overcome that were preventing us from merging as soulmates as should have been our romantic destiny. She couldn't risk the social consequences of making a public declaration of romantic intent toward me. That's why she had to hide her relationship from her friends and family, sneaking out to visit me for a weekend here and there in Karaköy, lying to everyone in her life about where she'd been while bonding with me. I was pre-disqualified on racial and cultural grounds as a suitable romantic partner for her because I didn't conform to her parents' and larger society's expectations for the singular condoned way her love life should unfold. My very existence in her life was a threat to their control because I influenced her with ideals of romantic self-determination.

But disclosure could not be delayed forever. When her parents learned the truth about what had been going on in her private life, their ideological immune system reared up into a full-blown ideollergic reaction,[35] like the body's defense mechanisms confronting an innocent particle of pollen that had entered its domain. A barrage of questions about the life I would decide for Zehra if they were to permit our unconventional pairing to continue erupted. Would we live far away from them? Would I, as a dangerous foreign agent, interfere with Zehra's obligations to and role within her family? Would I lessen the influence they had over their offspring? I reminded Zehra that, unlike her parents, I had no and would never seek any coercive authority over her, even as her husband. But it was too late. A threshold out of fantasy and into the real world had been crossed. Zehra could not go on pretending that she and I were the only people in the world and that differences in our cultures didn't matter. Now, it was time for us to confront the consequences of our romantic rebellion against the present social order.

---

35 *"Ideollergic reaction" is a neologistic portmanteau of "ideological allergic reaction."*

Witnessing how Zehra's parents interacted with her, I finally began to understand why she had broken down so many times when visiting me alone, visibly shaking from the fear that her parents might find out where she was and what she was doing. Only *their* agency mattered in her world. I asked her how she would feel if my family in America rejected her simply because her skin wasn't the right color or she didn't align with their idea of the woman I should marry. How hurtful would that be, to have the people closest to me make her seem less valuable in my eyes? She could not answer. Like Stockholm syndrome,[36] it was impossible for Zehra to cast her suppressors in a negative light. The more our relationship pulled her out of her restrictions, the more defensive she ultimately became of them. As an American, I could only think of stories I'd grown up hearing about how taboo the concept of interracial marriage between blacks and whites was just a few generations earlier in our nation. It's the kind of thing you grow up in the West thinking the human race had outgrown for its obvious idiocy and inhumanity—until you are directly confronted with it on both a personal and societal level, until it is the one thing preventing you from fulfilling your lifelong ambition of bonding with your soulmate.

Zehra, my soulmate, could no longer hide me away in a pocket universe, safe from the consequences of what she had been conditioned to think of as the real world, with restrictions on her romantic self-expression as immutable to her as the laws of physics. She was accountable for her actions now—the most terrifying experience in the world to her. I could no longer continue as her

---

36 *Stockholm syndrome is a psychological response in which victims form an emotional bond with their captors or abusers and defend their coercive actions. It has been observed in hostage situations, cults, human trafficking, domestic violence, child abuse, and prisoner-of-war camps as an unconscious coping strategy to minimize trauma.*

secret rogue boyfriend in an enslaved culture that would never permit my association with its protected royalty. The proverbial cat was out of the bag, and the cat was me. Now, she would be forced to make a choice about the person she was going to continue to be in the world shaped by her parents and those who came before her: a woman who would stand up for the right to express herself romantically the way she had always dreamed of, or one who would sacrifice her conscious self-expression to maintain the comfort she had always known. "There is a future," I told her, "where you and I are growing old together, where we have children and grandchildren and love each other deeply for the rest of our lives. That future depends on the choices you make now." It wasn't just her family I was fighting but her entire culture's collective associations and the judgment they would bring down upon anyone who dared to live differently, who embraced the freedom that a life with me represented.

And then, the most terrible thing that can happen to a romantic happened—something worse than being cheated on, worse than being abandoned by my oldest friend in the world, and even worse than being forgotten about by countless romantic partners prior. I saw the woman I loved, the most beautiful woman in the world to me, slowly turn into someone very ugly by descending to the point of embodying the very opposite of her romantic ideals. She began to treat me like a stranger she had never known so closely, easily agitated and in conscious denial, now internally framing our soulmate connection as something fabricated in my imagination—as though the whole relationship and everything we shared had never even happened. She was now a different person living in a different universe of her own design. Someone once so deep, complex, and meaningful regressed into a mostly shallow vessel without any of the original thought and passion that made her so attractive and such a natural soulmate for me. It felt like watching her growing old on her deathbed, ravaged by dementia à la Nicholas Sparks,[37] only occasionally returning to the surface of delusion to briefly remember and then cast out again from mind the truth of our miraculous connection.

Zehra became a stranger to me, too. Romantic love requires extreme discrimination. It is not, as commonly thought, *un*conditional but one of the *most* conditional states in the universe. I saw someone I still recognized, in a superficial sense, as a familiar face. But I also saw someone I did not know at all because all the conceptual qualities I assigned to that face had shifted into a state in complete contradiction to it. The physical beauty I perceived in her had only the smallest amount to do with how incredible she had looked to me and how happy and at peace I was in her presence. It was our miraculous compatibility that previously brought me to that state, that showed me that intangible ideal I had always been chasing. That, too, was now gone. I know that if I met Zehra now, with her acting the way she has regressed to since our time together, I would *not* be attracted to her. I would not even notice her among a sea of similarly anti-romantic women. We would form no bond. I can see this clearly despite the fact that I am still deeply bonded to the memory of the more fully expressed version of her I met years ago in secret. Right away, I saw someone I could get very close to in her. Shortly after, I saw someone I could

---

37 *In Sparks' The Notebook (Warner Books, 1996), Alzheimer's disease has destroyed the memory of aging Allie, including her entire history of meeting and falling in love with her husband Noah long ago. Noah strives to help her recall their past by posing as a stranger and reading the story of their love from a notebook, occasionally resulting in breakthroughs where Allie briefly remembers her overwhelming love for Noah. The 2004 movie adaptation faithfully portrays these events.*

spend my life with. Now, she's lost all those wonderful qualities I loved because she has stopped expressing the honest desires of her soul and become the worst version of herself, the version capable of doing monstrous things to others with a straight face.

One essential question on the nature of identity remains. Is the beautiful woman I remember who Zehra really was? Or was it only a detour from this uglier person she has allowed herself to become? Which version was real, and which was the imposter? The two cannot coexist in the same body because they are contradictory in values and actions.

I believe that Zehra is a romantic by nature whose consciousness has been deliberately suppressed by those who fear its power to disrupt their comfortable social order. Like so many women who were once eager to bond with me, she met me at a time when she was just barely becoming brave enough to attempt to step away from the restrictions forced upon her feminine self-expression, to question the inherited idea that there was something wrong with her for holding the highest romantic ideals that were practically without precedent in her society. She and I won the romantic lottery when we found each other. Hopeless romantics everywhere lament that they cannot accomplish what we did. But she allowed her world to make her afraid, to tell her she was wrong to pursue what she naturally desired as an element of her fullest self-expression and become more than what they knew her to be.

There is a psychological wall, a suppressive blanket that prevents all but the most confidently self-expressed from pursuing their grand romantic ambitions. That's every great love story ever told: two people fighting the established order to build a new one based on something deep and true to the lovers who are brave enough to be themselves, wholly embodied, in the face of everything working against them. Like so many other women in codependent family relationships, women who have been made to treat their parents as partners holding the reins to their soul, Zehra could not express her values in place of theirs. She could not establish her individuality because she would always prioritize a higher authority's values over her own, disabling her free will and ability to choose her own destiny because she would always be treated as a child by them until some proper, approved husband came along to play that same role in her life. She experienced a breakdown of authentic personality because she was put into a panic state that made her easier to control by those who sought to do so. Because of it, an entire future was lost. All the generations who would have been the product of our deep bonding will never come into this world, and we will never become the people we would have been under each other's complementary consciousness-enabling influence.

When people from different worlds come together, the new world they build is uncharted. There are no established structures for it. That's what makes it so romantic. It's a complete departure from the known and requires total trust in one another. That's why we tell love stories: to spread an ambition worth living up to in the real world. I know of no greater way to honor the would-be world that was destroyed between me and Zehra than to continue to be, against all resistance and to the best of my ability, the man she fell in love with—the man who, despite everything, remembers the truth and lives up to his ideals.

CHAPTER 7

Returning to the Void[38]

> "*Almost all of a man's sense of value, worth, safety, joy, contentment, belongingness, and happiness derive from his inner feminine nature... Happiness is feminine in a man, a feeling quality and generally mysterious to him.*"
>
> — Robert A. Johnson, *Lying with the Heavenly Woman*
> (HarperCollins, 1993)

I can remember all the parts of me that were desperate for the semblance of peace certain women brought me. I remember feeling that I could not go on with anything I invested myself into because so much of it was, ultimately, not for me but for some woman I adored. I remember the juvenile version of me that was so easily superstimulated, so easily motivated into action by attractive body parts and faces, pulled about in so many directions by superficial impulses. I think about the man I would have become had I stayed with each woman I bonded with, if I had merged my identity with each particular woman at different stages of development. I would have ceased maturing and integrated with the world on

---

38 *Or: Life Without a Happy Ending.*

the terms of the woman who acted as my doorway to it. I would have allowed myself to be happy with existence—just being, with no reason to face dragons, challenge myself, and grow.

In myth, a fair maiden or beautiful princess is a warrior's reward for storming castles, defeating dragons, and ultimately saving the world. Would he undertake all that hardship if there were no princess to rescue? Would he still be willing to better himself through struggle and injury from impossible but important undertakings? Is the quest itself still worth it without her? Maybe if he persists long enough, he'll find his life's great love, and his life will be beautiful ever after. But he cannot depend on that happening. And if he is only championing because of the anticipation of the relief that comes with reward, he is not virtuous or acting in integrity. He has to be the best man he can be under all possible circumstances—even walking through hell alone for all eternity, or at least so long as his flesh can endure. Being inspired by women is the first step for men; the last is no longer depending on them to be the men we are supposed to be.

After the loss of that connection, that being that appeared in our lives to save us from ourselves, it's incomprehensibly difficult to go on existing alone. You know how much better you are capable of being with the right woman complementing you. Navigating the cold alone again, a man is forced to grow deeper into himself, perhaps for many years longer than he ever thought he would. Without her, he is now displaced energy without a home to return to. But with her, his splintered pieces went where they belonged. He remembered everything he was capable of and what he was supposed to become. She was a gravity well for his attention and conviction. And when she is not part of his life anymore, he is in danger of growing bitter and disenchanted, ceasing to be useful to anyone.

To stay invested, he needs to find someone he will always want to share his experience of the world with, someone he can stand to be around, someone he will always look forward to being with, whose company he will always prefer to his own, someone who shows him the good of the world because he frequently doesn't see it on his own. Or maybe he doesn't deserve to rest yet or be happy. Maybe he has not earned the end of his trials. Perhaps this is how men turn into alienated mystics—all spirit and no flesh. Alone, almost nothing is worth sticking to. Nothing can slow it all down and allow the disconnected man to see the beauty and detail in things that other people take for granted. Nothing gives him an organic sense of belonging in the too-big and too-detailed world—nothing like *her*. Perhaps it is a futile pursuit, and he will only end up injuring himself while chasing the beauty that is absent in his soul. He will only fall in love with women who share his vision to the extent it is convenient and entertaining for them. That is hell on Earth for a man: to be drawn by his nature into that which will only destroy him.

It is the greatest test of a man's character to not let the bitterness of disconnect overtake him, to remain true to his ideals even when he is not rewarded for dedication to his cause. He is only a fraction as effective operating on his own, but he must act anyway. He must remain faithful to who he is, or else he will always be subject to externalities he cannot control. He will always depend on something he can lose. Concretes, flesh-and-blood women who embody the principle of femininity, can always be lost. Man's connection to the world has to come from something intangible and representative of more, or else we operate from a very fragile position. The more captivating we find individual women, the more of ourselves we place in their hands and the more we have to lose.

It takes a very determined and idealistic man to have been through the hell of his disappointed ideals and still willfully pursue them. Still, questions remain that any self-honest individual must be willing to confront: What have I been doing wrong? Is there something wrong with me, my standards, my strategy, or the women I select (and who I allow to select me) as objects of affection? Perhaps the idealist's entire paradigm of intimacy, sex, and love is incompatible with the world around him. But that does not mean that his ideals are wrong and that he should not continue to be who he is to the furthest extent possible.

I've certainly never been perfect toward any woman I've loved, but I've learned and improved based on what I could have done better to integrate the lessons of past failures. What sticks out to me is a series of women who pretended to be ready for greater intimacy than they were. I see immature minds that dabbled in romanticism without considering the responsibility of it. At the foundational level, every woman I have loved has been a fearful and conflicted being of competing personas—and I am guilty of expecting consistency with what they promised to become in our projected future. It would have been foolish of me to bond with any temporary state of a woman and become disappointed when she grew into something else. The key was loving the principle of who they were and setting an intentional trajectory for change with them.

When we consciously bond, we are agreeing to change with someone in a way befitting us both. We are making a promise about who we are, who we will continue to be, who we will become, and even who we will *never* let ourselves be. It is *necessary* for intimate partners to expect each other to change, even to help each other change in the best ways possible with the complementary influence offered to and received from one another. Partners hold each other accountable to the standards they have set independently and together. Their fundamental nature. Their sense of ethics. The state of their relationship and obligations to each other. What roles they play in each other's lives. It is the only way to grow together instead of apart. The error lies in projecting a trajectory for someone because it is what *we* wish to see in them instead of what *they* consciously choose for themselves as an application of their highest ideals. Now, I only expect the changes the women who enter my life communicate that I should expect from them.

If we cannot trust who the people we care about tell us they are, a sustainable bond is impossible. How can I invest in you and undertake great challenges to be with you if I don't know who I'm doing it for—if I don't know who you might be tomorrow? A serious relationship is a wake-up call to being accountable. People realize, maybe for the first time in their lives, that they can't just act however they want anymore. Someone close to them is depending on them to play a certain role in their life, and there are consequences for failing to fulfill that expectation. I know how big the expectations I've set for the women I've loved have been, but I've never set them alone. The future I envisioned for us was in line with what they communicated as their deepest values, too.

Idealists are notoriously naïve. We see the world as what it *could* and *should* be, not only what it *happens* to be *right now*. There were so many times I should have walked away from women sooner than I did. I can pinpoint exact moments, in some cases, when I had enough evidence to reach the conclusion that our relationship was unsustainable. I kick myself for not acting differently in those moments when I should have known better than to keep trying. I had to learn to commit to decisiveness in the face of inconsistency so that I wouldn't be left vulnerable to people who wouldn't return the same courtesies I extended them. No matter how compatible it seems we are, no matter how much chemistry there is, no matter how hot the sex is… without consistency of thought and action, there is no foundation. All forward momentum stops if I do not know who to expect them to be tomorrow.

I still believe romantic love could and should be easy. Two people could just come together as soon as they see they are romantically compatible. When two people feel good around each other… when they want to see and talk to each other every day… when they naturally move their bodies closer whenever the opportunity allows… romantic bonding should be the obvious, nearly automatic result. This turns into passionate sex and the merging of concerns, lifestyles, and identities if they stay the course together—even the merging of biology into the procreation of new life. Of all the worries and anxieties that come with starting a family, only one has ever mattered to me: that of who I would bond with, who I would combine myself with, in the most literal sense, to create life, and who would caretake, protect, and prepare that life with me. It has also been crucial to me that just as I have expected the woman I bring children into the world with to be the best, fully self-expressed version of herself before undertaking the task with me so that she may be the best possible wife and mother, I too must ensure that I have done everything in my power to ensure I am the man who meets my own standards for how a father should be to his children.

My father was a good provider. Maybe even a great one. I can't fault him at all for his ability to put food on the table and occupy his children with extracurricular activities. But when I look back on my childhood memories, what stands out most is how much he failed to embody the mythological role of father in my developing psyche as more than just a provider. It seems that everything I learned from him happened more by accident than intention. I can scarcely remember a time when he sat down and explained how something worked,[39] what kind of man I should want to become, or how to actually succeed in that existential quest. But I know that "teacher" and "mentor" are some of the most important roles that fall under the umbrella category of "father," alongside "protector" and "provider." Upon reflection, I accepted that I did not have parents in more than a biological sense. Mythologically, I was an orphan stranded in space, floating through the cosmos alone, having committed spiritual patricide much younger than most boys do. It was as though my consciousness popped into this world without an origin point (a mythological mother) or an example of what it was supposed to become (a mythological father). Because of that, I know what role I will need to play for my own children as their father in more than just blood and resources.

If a man's ambition is to procreate, he must factor into his romantic choice that his feminine partner will one day be the mother of his children. But these are not exclusive categories. Her propensity for motherhood should be an extension of the same natural feminine qualities he is attracted to in her, just as his for fatherhood is an extension of his natural masculinity. Their romantic chemistry with one another should extend into the act of childrearing. How they influence each other as the primary masculine and feminine romantic forces, respectively, in each other's lives also influences how they will play their masculine

---

39 *There was actually one half-hearted attempt from my father at a sex talk, which came much later than would have been useful and amounted to little more than "Women think about sex very differently than men, so you have to be careful with them." Good advice, for what it's worth.*

and feminine parental roles in their children's lives. How they do everything else together will be how they raise children, too. A mother and father with poor romantic chemistry will always do a worse job than they could at raising their children because they will be worse versions of themselves, not fully self-expressed. An exhausted father will not have the beauty that brings him peace, and a neurotic mother will not have the structure to give her a fundamental sense of security.

A funny thing happened after my parents divorced when I was a young man and my father remarried quickly with the woman he left my mother for. I was able to observe my father slowly evolve into a state of manhood in his elder years absent from all my childhood memories of my parents together and ostensibly in love. He grew into a calmer, more peaceful man than I had known growing up. He must have recognized, on some level, that he made a mistake marrying, procreating with, and rearing children in a relationship with a woman who fit him well on paper but who did not bring essential feminine light into his life. It was enough to make me wonder how different of a father, how different of a man, he might have been under other romantic and parenting circumstances. Men will sacrifice everything for that peace—even decades of marriage and family by pursuing someone who appears more capable of offering it. My mother, meanwhile, never seemed to recover from a general sense of insecurity and unease after my father left. She never met the man who would give her safety. My father had failed to fully play his romantic role in her life as much as she had hers in his.

And what if a man should lose the mother of his children and have to continue raising their offspring alone? Will it be enough for him to persist as a solitary father without their mother as his and their primary feminine influence? The concrete can always be lost, so he cannot ever fully rely on her. If he is going to be responsible for the upbringing of children and exist as their mythological father figure, he needs to feel invested in the world for the long term. Anything less would not be fair to them. The moment he becomes responsible for them is the moment he gives up the freedom to detach from whatever is not serving him and retreat into the cosmic void. As their father, he will be undertaking an oath to fight for them and their future. If he is in love with the woman he creates life with, his soulmate, their children will be extensions of the root she gives him into the Earth's soil. They will be his love for and connection to her embodied.

Romanticism of this depth would be easier in societal conditions that allowed for fuller self-expression. Our world breeds people riddled with insecurities, resulting in underexplored and underexpressed aspects of their identities, preventing them from confidently embodying who they are in the romantic domain. Romanticism, true romanticism, occurs as a conscious rebellion against a broken world. It's a heroic act of defiance and a revolution of the heart against suppression. Most people have never been that willingly vulnerable with anyone. Our most intimate relationships are often unconscious or coercive, born out of cultural obligation rather than because we love and care of our own volition as an expression of who we are.

As it stands, the romantic man cannot depend on the world to provide him the feminine influence he needs in the miraculous form of the right woman, hoping he will somehow be lucky enough to pair with his soulmate so that he might become and remain the man he is supposed to be. What does he do when there's no princess waiting in the castle? He slays the dragon anyway. We are so accustomed to seeing the peace a woman brings as the incentive, the reward structure for doing difficult (maybe even impossible) but important things that no other man could. We forget we should be doing them anyway, for our own sake. So he slays, again and again, every day, even if there's *never* a princess. So long as he's doing it for some woman's sake, his choices will be shaped by what he thinks will impress her, not what is in integrity with the truth of his identity. Without a woman, he fights only because he knows it is important and right. He forgets about the promise of heaven for his good deeds on Earth. *His* analysis is what matters, even if it's him versus the world forever. It is a reward entirely localized to and contained within himself, his little spaceship afloat in the cosmic void, and not subject to externalities; thus, it cannot ever be taken from him.

Romantic women, too, must learn to be beautiful in an ugly world where they cannot always get what they need from men who fail to live up to their ideals. If they cannot learn to feel fundamentally secure in themselves, they may become desperate to partner with any remotely masculine force the wind blows into their lives, especially as they get older. A single man's highest priority becomes finding comfort because he is so miserable on his own, which means he cannot focus on developing his masculine superpowers and virtues and applying them in pursuit of what he cares about. A single woman's highest priority becomes defending and taking care of herself, protecting her emotional state in the way she would normally expect a man to. She cannot flourish in providing the color and beauty she is born to. Neither can live up to their potential and offer their gifts to the world until they decide to be the best they can be even when the world does not give them what they need.

Anyway, women are more attracted to men that they see persevering in spite of everything going against them, in spite of getting nothing in return for their struggle. Developed women seek stability and consistency of character. Developed men send out signals that attract the right women, retiring from going on the hunt for them simply because they look and smell enticing. A man can learn to be more like a woman, so to speak. The man who willingly faces hell alone is unstoppable—and sexy as fuck to the woman who matters. He must choose his next connection to life very wisely.

If you ever feel that you are lost in the world without the woman or women who once gave you a semblance of belonging, remember what it was that you loved about them. Remember the principle of the beauty you saw represented by them. Those feelings did not come from nowhere. They are central to who you are and your experience of the world. Even those you have lost to physical death or distance or those who have become the worst versions of themselves and stopped putting their feminine virtues out into the world can carry on in your memory for what good they once offered. Remember what you loved about every woman who disappointed you, who failed to live up to her potential and embody who she should have been. Those qualities were real. A better world, where those qualities thrive, is possible. You know now, without a doubt, that you are capable of loving and bonding deeply, capable of experiencing profound joy and beauty when once it might have seemed impossible for you. That much is true. The principle of feminine virtue remains present somewhere in this cold world. So long as you continue to live with that awareness, you will be a far more complete, capable, heroic, and exceptional version of yourself, embodying your masculine virtues.

Social change, true revolution and the evolution of how the world turns, begins with individuals who are not afraid to think, feel, and act for themselves according to the passions that burn within them as products of their nature. The inclination toward romantic love is potentially the strongest passion human beings are capable of. The fuel supply can never run out so long as romantics do not let the world suppress them or make them feel ashamed for being what they are: idealists regarding one of the most important human experiences. Why should we be made to believe there is something wrong with us for being what we are, for having the highest standards and pulling society ever-so-slightly closer toward a more tolerable, loving, and humanitarian state where people are finally free to express themselves? I will believe what I believe for as long as it is physically possible, for as long as my flesh persists, and I will not be shy about upholding it as a worthwhile ideal. Seeking the fullest possible ethical self-expression will always be the highest good for humanity.

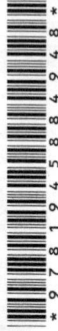